CONTENTS

BREAKFASTS

BACON - TWO WAYS

Use this seasoning to make crunchy bacon bits, perfect to use as a topping, or to create crispy strips to serve at breakfast. Make sure to use the rice wrappers you would use for summer rolls, not the wafer kind.

Serves 4
Preparation time: 15 minutes
Cooking time: 15 minutes

BACON BITS

2 tbsp olive oil
1 tbsp soy sauce
1 tbsp balsamic vinegar
1 tbsp maple syrup
1 tsp smoked paprika
½ tsp sea salt
100g/3½oz (2 cups) flaked coconut

1. Preheat the oven to 130°C fan/150°C/300°F/gas 2.
2. Mix the oil, soy sauce, vinegar, maple syrup, paprika and salt together in a large bowl and stir in the coconut flakes, mixing until completely coated.
3. Transfer the coconut to a baking tray and spread into a thin even layer. Bake for 10–15 minutes until crispy, stirring the flakes every 5 minutes to ensure even cooking. The bacon bits can be kept for up to 3 weeks in an airtight container.

CRISPY BACON STRIPS

2 tbsp olive oil
1 tbsp soy sauce
1 tbsp balsamic vinegar
1 tbsp maple syrup
1 tsp smoked paprika
½ tsp sea salt
4 sheets rice wrapers

1. Preheat the oven to 180°C fan/200°C/400°F/gas 6 and line a large baking tray with greaseproof paper.
2. Mix the oil, soy sauce, vinegar, maple syrup, paprika and salt together in a shallow dish.
3. Stack two sheets of the rice paper on top of one another and soak in a bowl of cold water briefly to soften them. Using kitchen scissors, cut the sheets into bacon-sized strips.
4. Dip each strip into the mixture, coating the paper on each side, before laying on the prepared baking tray. Use a pastry brush, dipped into the mixture, to give them a second coating on the baking tray.
5. Bake for 5–8 minutes, watching carefully to make sure they don't burn. They should be crispy and textured with a good crunch. Serve immediately as they will lose their crunch after a few hours.

FULL ENGLISH

Serves 2
Preparation time: 20 minutes
Cooking time: 25 minutes

*Weekends aren't the same without a fry-up.
This vegan version will cure your cravings and
is packed with plant-based protein and fibre.*

2–4 Vegan Sausages (see page 63)
1 tbsp vegetable oil
8 cherry tomatoes
2 large flat mushrooms, stalks
    removed and peeled
1 x 400g/14oz can baked beans
2 handfuls of spinach, washed
1 tbsp balsamic vinegar
8 Crispy Bacon Strips (see page 15)
1 recipe quantity Tofu Scramble (opposite)
    or 2 Vegan Fried Eggs (see page 32)
sea salt and ground black pepper
buttered toast, to serve

1. Preheat the grill to medium–high. Put the vegan
   sausages in a large roasting tray and drizzle with
   the oil. Grill for 10 minutes, then turn the sausages
   and add the tomatoes and mushrooms. Cook for
   5–8 minutes. Turn the grill off but leave the tray
   under it to keep everything warm.
2. In a small saucepan, warm the baked beans for
   5 minutes over a low–medium heat.
3. Place the spinach, the balsamic vinegar and a splash
   of water in a small saucepan. Put the lid on and cook
   for 2 minutes over a medium heat, until the spinach
   has wilted.
4. Divide the spinach between the plates followed by
   the beans, sausages, tomatoes, mushrooms, bacon
   and tofu scramble or fried eggs. Season with salt and
   pepper and serve with buttered toast.

TOFU SCRAMBLE

Serves 4
Preparation time: 5 minutes
Cooking time: 10 minutes

1 tbsp dairy-free butter
1 x 396g/14oz block of firm tofu, drained
¼ tsp kala namak (black salt)
1 tsp ground turmeric
a pinch of ground black pepper
a few drops of unsweetened dairy-
    free milk (optional)
fresh chives, chopped (optional), to serve

This scramble tastes just like the real deal, especially if you can get hold of some black salt, which adds an eggy flavour. It's delicious served on toast or as part of a full English breakfast.

1. Heat the butter in a frying pan and then crumble the tofu into small pieces before adding to the pan.
2. Add the black salt, turmeric and pepper and cook for 7 minutes. Pour in a little milk if you want a creamier consistency.
3. To serve, add some extra ground black pepper and sprinkle with a few chopped chives, if you like.

LEFTOVERS BUBBLE AND SQUEAK

Serves 4
Preparation time: 10 minutes
Cooking time: 20 minutes

3 tbsp vegetable oil
1 onion, diced
about 500g/1lb 2oz leftover
    mashed potatoes, or
    roasted potatoes blitzed
    in a food processor
about 150g/5½oz leftover
    cooked cabbage or
    Brussels sprouts
plain (all-purpose) flour,
    for dusting
sea salt and ground
    black pepper
ketchup, to serve (optional)

An extremely versatile recipe that makes the most of Sunday lunch or Christmas dinner leftovers, making it the best Boxing Day breakfast. I prefer to make small patties that can either be baked or fried as it is easier for serving, but you can also cook it all together in the pan, the traditional way.

1. Heat 1 tablespoon of the oil in a large frying pan over a low–medium heat and fry the onion for 5 minutes, until softened. Remove the pan from the heat.
2. Pour the cooked onion into a large mixing bowl, along with the rest of the vegetables. Mash well to combine and season with salt and pepper.
3. Lightly dust your hands with flour and shape the mixture into eight patties.
4. Add the remaining oil to the frying pan you cooked the onion in and put over a high heat, allowing the oil to get hot for a minute or so. Once hot, fry the patties, cooking for 2 minutes on each side until golden brown, gently pressing down with a spatula as they cook. (You can also bake them for 25 minutes in an oven at 180°C fan/200°C/400°F/gas 6, if preferred.)
5. Serve the bubble and squeak patties on their own with ketchup, or as part of a big breakfast with vegan sausages and beans.

CARROT CAKE MUESLI

Serves 2
Preparation time: 5 minutes

70g/2½oz (⅔ cup) rolled oats
½ tsp ground cinnamon
1 tbsp ground flaxseed
4 tbsp raisins
½ medium carrot, peeled and grated
2 tbsp dessicated (dried shredded) coconut
25g/1oz (¼ cup) chopped walnuts
500ml/17fl oz dairy-free milk, to serve
golden syrup (light corn syrup),
    to serve (optional)

This muesli tastes just like carrot cake batter, which is great news if you crave dessert for breakfast! It is so easy to prepare and is full of nutritional goodness too. It also works as a bircher museli: simply prepare as described, adding the milk, and leave in a container in the fridge overnight, ready to serve in the morning.

1. Simply mix the oats, cinnamon, flaxseed, raisins, carrot, coconut and walnuts together and divide into two bowls.
2. Serve with milk and, if you want it a bit sweeter, a dollop of golden syrup.

ENGLISH PANCAKES

Makes 8
Preparation time: 5 minutes
Cooking time: 20 minutes

200g/7oz (1½ cups) plain
    (all-purpose) flour
1 tsp baking powder
1 tbsp caster sugar
1 tbsp vegetable oil
450ml/16fl oz (2 cups)
    unsweetened dairy-
    free milk
dairy-free butter, for frying
your choice of topping, to serve

These pancakes can be made sweet or savoury, depending on which toppings you desire. I personally love the classic sprinkling of sugar and a squeeze of lemon.

1. Sift the flour into a large bowl and mix in the baking powder and sugar.
2. Pour in the oil, then slowly whisk in the milk in a steady stream, to avoid lumps, until you have a smooth batter.
3. Add a teaspoon of butter to a medium-sized frying pan over a medium heat. Once it starts to sizzle, pour a ladleful of the batter into the pan, swirling quickly to evenly coat the bottom.
4. Cook for 30 seconds, or until the edge of the pancake starts to curl away from the side of the pan. Carefully use a spatula to flip the pancake onto the other side. If you prefer a bit of showmanship, use the spatula to just loosen the edges, before flipping it yourself! Cook on the other side for another 30 seconds or so, then transfer to a plate and repeat to use up the rest of the batter, adding more butter if needed.
5. Serve the pancakes, rolled up or folded into quarters, with your choice of topping.

SCOTCH PANCAKES

Makes 6 pancakes
Preparation time: 5 minutes
Cooking time: 6 minutes

90g/3¼oz (⅔ cup) self-raising
    (self-rising) flour
1 tbsp cornflour (cornstarch)
½ tsp baking powder
3 tbsp golden syrup
    (light corn syrup)
1 tsp apple cider vinegar
120ml/4fl oz (½ cup)
    unsweetened dairy-
    free milk
2 tbsp vegetable oil

To serve
dairy-free butter (optional)
your favourite jam (optional)

If you prefer the thicker, fluffier variety of pancakes, these Scotch-style ones will hit the spot. Stack them up and top with some melted dairy-free butter or a generous dollop of jam.

1. Heat a large non-stick frying pan over a low heat (you don't need any oil for this).
2. Mix the flour, cornflour and baking powder together in a bowl.
3. Combine the golden syrup, vinegar and milk in a large jug. Pour the liquid into the flour mixture and whisk together until well combined and the mixture is runny but thick.
4. Ladle approximately 4 tablespoons of the batter per pancake into the pan (I usually cook three at a time) and allow to cook for 20–30 seconds, or until bubbles start to form on top. Carefully flip the pancakes and cook for another 20–30 seconds. Remove from the pan and repeat to cook the rest of the batter.
5. Serve immediately topped with the butter or jam.

CRUMPETS

Makes 10
Preparation time: 15
minutes, plus proving
Cooking time: 20 minutes

380ml/13fl oz (generous
    1½ cups) unsweetened
    dairy-free milk
1 tbsp fast-action dried yeast
1 tsp caster sugar
240g/8½oz (1¾ cups)
    strong white flour
a pinch of sea salt
½ tsp bicarbonate of soda
    (baking soda)
vegetable oil, for cooking
jam or dairy-free butter, to serve

I didn't think I liked crumpets until I tried making my own and found that it really makes the difference! Now I am a huge fan and regularly eat them for breakfast, especially since they are so much simpler to make than I thought.

1. Put the milk in a small saucepan and warm very gently over a low heat. Remove from the heat, pour into a bowl and add 100ml/3½fl oz tepid water, the yeast and the sugar. Leave in a warm place for 15 minutes to allow the yeast to dissolve and become frothy.
2. In another large bowl, mix the flour, salt and bicarbonate of soda. Make a well in the centre and whisk in the yeast mixture until you have a creamy consistency. Cover the bowl with a slightly damp towel and let it rest for an hour until you start to see bubbles form on the surface.
3. Grease a set of crumpet or egg rings and the base of a large frying pan with some oil. Arrange the rings in the pan and set over a medium heat. Once hot, add about 4 tablespoons of the batter into each ring and cook for 5 minutes, until little holes start to appear on top. Carefully, using tongs, remove the rings and turn the crumpets over. Cook for a further 1–2 minutes. Remove from the pan and keep warm while you repeat to cook the rest of the batter.
4. Serve warm with some jam or butter.

DIPPY SOLDIERS

Serves 4
Preparation time: 5 minutes
Cooking time: 5 minutes

250ml/9fl oz (1 cup) unsweetened
    dairy-free milk
1½ tbsp cornflour (cornstarch)
1 tbsp mild olive oil
¼ tsp kala namak (black salt) or sea salt
1 tbsp nutritional yeast flakes
a pinch of ground black pepper
¼ tsp ground turmeric
4 slices of toast, to serve
dairy-free butter, to serve

*What British child didn't grow up loving this
breakfast? But of course, adults love it too and
this plant-based version is just as delicious and
fun to eat.*

1. In a small saucepan, combine all the ingredients,
   except the turmeric. Bring the mixture to a boil
   over a high heat, then lower to a medium heat
   and whisk for about 3 minutes, until the mixture
   thickens. It should be smooth and glossy.
2. Remove the mixture from the heat and stir in the
   turmeric. Pour into egg cups or small glasses.
3. Butter the toast and cut into soldiers. Serve
   immediately.

WELSH CAKES

Makes 10
Preparation time: 20 minutes
Cooking time: 15 minutes

225g/8oz/1¾ cups self-
    raising flour (self-rising),
    plus extra for dusting
75g/2½oz/½ cup raisins
¼ tsp ground mixed spice
    (apple pie spice)
½ tsp ground cinnamon
75g/2½oz/⅓ cup caster
    sugar (superfine), plus
    extra for dusting
100g/3½oz/7 tbsp dairy-
    free butter
50ml/1¾fl oz/3½ tbsp
    unsweetened dairy-free milk
1 tsp vegetable oil

These have been a popular British teatime treat since the late nineteenth century. I like them best at breakfast as they're wonderful served warm from the pan with dairy-free butter, or just by themselves later on in the afternoon.

1. In a large bowl, combine the flour, raisins, mixed spice, cinnamon and sugar. Add the butter and rub into the flour with the tips of your fingers until you have a breadcrumb consistency.
2. Make a well in the centre and pour in the milk. Gently stir until a dough is formed.
3. Sprinkle a work surface with some flour and roll out the dough to ½cm/¼in thickness. Use cookie cutters to cut out 5cm/2in discs. You should be able to get about ten from the dough.
4. Heat the oil in a frying pan over a medium heat. Fry the cakes, in batches, for 2 minutes on each side, until golden brown.
5. Remove from the pan and sprinkle with extra sugar. Serve immediately or store in an airtight container for up to 3 days.

BREAKFAST BUTTY

Serves 2
Preparation time: 10 minutes
Cooking time: 5 minutes

For the vegan fried egg
45g/1½oz (1/3 cup) gram
    flour (chickpea flour)
a pinch of kala namak (black
    salt) or sea salt
a pinch of ground black pepper
vegetable oil, for frying

For the butty
2 soft white rolls
2 tsp dairy-free butter
2 cooked Vegan Sausages
    (see page 63)
1 recipe quantity of Crispy
    Bacon Strips (see page 15)
2 tbsp brown sauce

*A bacon and egg butty might be the kind of thing
you'd expect to never have again after going
plant-based, but this version really hits the spot.
It has all the familiar flavour and texture for a
super-satisfying breakfast.*

1. First, make the fried egg by adding the gram
   flour to a small bowl and slowly whisking in
   120ml/4fl oz/½ cup water, along with the salt
   and pepper.
2. Lightly grease a frying pan with oil and turn the heat
   up to high. Once really hot, pour the mixture into
   the pan to create a couple of fried egg shapes. You
   can use greased crumpet or egg rings to help retain
   a thicker shape, if you wish. Cook for 1–2 minutes on
   each side until set.
3. To assemble the butties, halve and butter each roll.
   Slice the vegan sausages in half lengthways and
   place on the bottom half, then add the fried egg, top
   with a few bacon strips and a tablespoon of brown
   sauce. Sandwich with the other half of the roll.
   Repeat to fill the other roll and serve with a cuppa.

SOUPS & SALADS

CARROT AND CORIANDER SOUP

Serves 6
Preparation time: 8 minutes
Cooking time: 25 minutes

Light, aromatic and healthy, but oh so satisfying, this soup is perfect for winter or spring. Serve with some fresh crusty bread.

1 tbsp vegetable oil
1 white onion, roughly chopped
3 garlic cloves, crushed
½ tsp ground coriander
1 medium sweet potato,
    peeled and diced
400g/14oz carrots,
    peeled and sliced
1 litre/35fl oz/4¼ cups
    vegetable stock
a large handful of fresh
    coriander (cilantro), plus
    extra leaves, to garnish
sea salt and ground
    black pepper
crusty bread, to serve

1. Heat the oil in a large saucepan and sauté the onion for 3 minutes, until softened. Add the garlic and ground coriander and cook for a further 2 minutes.
2. Add the sweet potato, carrots and vegetable stock. Bring to the boil, then reduce to a simmer and cook for 15–20 minutes, or until the vegetables are tender.
3. Tip everything into a blender, add the fresh coriander and blitz until smooth. Season to taste and serve sprinkled with some extra fresh coriander leaves and ground black pepper.

MULLIGATAWNY

Serves 6
Preparation time: 10 minutes
Cooking time: 35 minutes

2 tbsp vegetable oil
1 red onion, diced
1 red (bell) pepper,
    deseeded and diced
2 medium carrots, peeled
    and diced
1 medium sweet potato,
    peeled and diced
3 garlic cloves, crushed
1 red chilli, finely chopped
a thumb-sized piece of ginger,
    peeled and finely chopped
½ tsp ground cumin
2 tbsp medium curry powder
1 tbsp balsamic vinegar
1 medium red apple,
    peeled and grated
1 x 400g/14oz can of chickpeas,
    drained and rinsed
100g/3½oz/heaped ½ cup
    dried red lentils
2 tbsp tomato purée (paste)
1.5 litres/52fl oz (6½ cups)
    vegetable stock
190g/6¾oz (heaped
    1 cup) basmati rice
sea salt and ground black pepper
coriander (cilantro)
    leaves, to serve

This recipe is a marriage between British and Indian ingredients to create a wholesome but spicy soup that is full of flavour. I have found it to be one of the best things for a cold or when you need a pick-me-up.

1. Heat the oil in a large saucepan and add the onion, pepper, carrots, sweet potato, garlic, chilli and ginger. Cook over a medium heat for about 10 minutes, until the vegetables begin to soften. Stir in the cumin, curry powder, balsamic vinegar and apple and cook for a further 2 minutes.
2. Add the chickpeas, lentils, tomato purée and vegetable stock. Bring to the boil, then simmer for 20 minutes.
3. Meanwhile, fill another saucepan with water and cook the rice for 10 minutes, or until tender. Drain and rinse under cold water.
4. Once the soup has had it's time and the vegetables are tender, you can leave the soup chunky or blend until smooth. I sometimes like to blend half so it's somewhere in-between. Season with salt and pepper to taste. Serve with a portion of the cooked rice and topped with some fresh coriander leaves and more black pepper.

CHEESY PEA SOUP

Serves 6
Preparation time: 10 minutes
Cooking time: 20 minutes

This is the soup I crave and make most often. Something about the combination of the sweet peas and the earthy, cheesy flavour makes it so moreish.

1 tbsp vegetable oil
1 white onion, roughly chopped
1 celery stick, roughly chopped
1 leek, roughly chopped
450g/1lb (3 cups) frozen
    petit pois
800ml/28fl oz (3½ cups)
    vegetable stock, plus
    extra if needed
50g/1¾oz (scant ½ cup)
    cashews, soaked for at least
    an hour in warm water
1 tsp yeast extract or
    miso paste
1 tbsp apple cider vinegar
3 tbsp nutritional yeast flakes
⅛ tsp ground nutmeg
sea salt and ground
    black pepper
Cashew Cream (see page 189)
    or soy yoghurt, to serve

1. Heat the oil in a large saucepan over a low-medium heat and sauté the onion, celery and leek for 8 minutes, until softened.
2. Add the peas, vegetable stock and cashews. Raise the heat to high and bring to the boil, then reduce the heat to medium and simmer for 2 minutes.
3. Pour the mixture into a blender, along with the yeast extract or miso paste, vinegar, nutritional yeast flakes and nutmeg, and blend until smooth, adding more vegetable stock if needed. Season to taste.
4. Serve with a swirl of cashew cream or soy yoghurt and sprinkle with a generous amount of black pepper to serve.

PUMPKIN, APPLE AND GINGER SOUP

Serves 4–6
Preparation time: 10 minutes
Cooking time: 45 minutes

500g/1lb 2oz pumpkin or
    squash, peeled, deseeded
    and chopped into chunks
2 Gala apples, peeled,
    cored and quartered
1 red onion, peeled
    and quartered
a thumb-sized piece of
    ginger, peeled
3 garlic cloves
1 tbsp olive oil
½ tsp ground mixed spice
    (apple pie spice)
500ml/17fl oz/2 cups vegetable
    stock, plus extra if needed
1 tbsp apple cider vinegar
sea salt and ground black pepper
dairy-free cream or
    yoghurt, to serve
fresh chives, roughly
    chopped, to serve

*A subtle sweetness from the pumpkin and apples,
paired with the gentle spice of the ginger makes
this an ultra-cosy, autumn meal.*

1. Preheat the oven to 180°C fan/200°C/400°F/gas 6 and
   add the pumpkin, apples, onion, ginger and garlic to a
   large roasting tray. Drizzle with the olive oil, sprinkle
   over the mixed spice and season with salt and pepper.
   Gently toss everything together to coat, then roast for
   30–40 minutes until golden.
2. Once cooked, unpeel the roasted garlic cloves and
   add them to a blender with the rest of the cooked
   ingredients and the vegetable stock and vinegar. Blend
   until smooth, adding more stock if needed.
3. Ladle the soup into bowls and swirl a dollop of cream
   or yoghurt on top of each one. Sprinkle with some
   chopped chives and serve.

CORONATION CHICKPEA SALAD

Serves 4

Preparation time: 10 minutes

1 x 400g/14oz can of chickpeas,
    drained and rinsed
4 tbsp Vegan Mayonnaise (see
    page 194) or plain yoghurt
2 tbsp mango chutney
1 tsp mild curry powder
½ tsp white (distilled) vinegar
½ tsp garlic granules
a pinch of sea salt
25g/1oz (scant ¼ cup) raisins
25g/1oz (¼ cup) flaked
    (sliced) almonds
a small handful of coriander
    (cilantro) leaves,
    roughly torn
2 heads of little gem (bibb)
    lettuce, leaves separated
    and washed, to serve

A royal British classic that can be prepared in just ten minutes. Creamy, sweet and spicy, this salad is packed with flavour and can be served on it's own, in lettuce 'cups', or makes an amazing sandwich.

1. Put the chickpeas, mayonnaise or yoghurt, chutney, curry powder, vinegar, garlic granules and salt into a large mixing bowl and, using a potato masher, roughly mash and mix together until half the chickpeas are crushed and the rest are left whole, for a chunky texture. Stir in the raisins, almonds and coriander leaves.
2. Spoon the salad into lettuce leaves to serve them in little 'cups'. Alternatively, shred the lettuce and mix it into the salad and serve in a bowl.

SQUASH, KALE AND LENTIL SALAD

Serves 4–6
Preparation time: 10 minutes
Cooking time: 30 minutes

500g/1lb 2oz butternut squash,
    peeled and diced
2 tbsp olive oil
¼ tsp dried chilli (hot pepper)
    flakes (optional)
1 tbsp balsamic vinegar
2 garlic cloves, crushed
100g/3½oz kale, washed, stems
    removed and roughly torn
1 x 400g/14oz can Puy lentils,
    drained and rinsed
sea salt and ground black pepper
Cashew Cheese Sauce (see
    page 189), to serve

This salad can be served hot or cold and makes a really hearty, autumn meal. It's also delicious served in a wrap with hummus.

1. Preheat the oven to 180°C fan/200°C/400°F/gas 6. Add the squash to a large roasting tray with 1 tablespoon of the olive oil and the chilli flakes, if using. Toss to coat, then roast for 25 minutes.
2. Meanwhile, add the remaining oil, vinegar and garlic to a large saucepan and stir in the kale. Put the lid on top and cook it over a low heat for 2 minutes, until wilted.
3. Remove the kale from the heat and stir in the lentils and roasted squash. Season with salt and pepper. Serve immediately warm or chilled with a drizzle of cashew cheese sauce.

MINTY PEA AND NEW POTATO SALAD

Serves 4–6
Preparation time: 10 minutes
Cooking time: 25 minutes

500g/1lb 2oz baby potatoes
2 tbsp dairy-free butter
200g/7oz (1½ cups) frozen peas
1 tbsp balsamic vinegar
a small bunch of fresh mint
    leaves, finely chopped
a small bunch of fresh chives,
    finely chopped
sea salt and ground black pepper

A fresh but satisfying salad that can be served warm or chilled. This makes the perfect barbecue side dish, if the weather allows it.

1. Add a pinch of salt to a large saucepan of water and bring to the boil. Cook the potatoes for 20 minutes, or until tender, then drain and leave to the side.
2. Add the butter to the pan and cook the peas over a medium heat for 2–3 minutes until heated through.
3. Remove the pan from the heat and add the rest of the ingredients, including the cooked potatoes, gently tossing everything together to coat. Season to taste and serve immediately whilst warm or chilled.

SPRING SALAD WITH SHAVED ASPARAGUS

Serves 4
Preparation time: 15 minutes

200g/7oz asparagus
3 spring onions (scallions),
    finely sliced
4 radishes
¼ cucumber
2 tbsp olive oil
1 tbsp balsamic vinegar
2 tbsp lemon juice
sea salt and ground black pepper

A refreshing green salad to celebrate spring's produce. This makes a great side dish or filling for a wrap, providing lots of crunch.

1. Use a vegetable peeler to shave the asparagus spears lengthways into thin strips. Add to a large bowl along with the spring onions.
2. Using a mandolin or small sharp knife, cut the radishes and cucumber into very thin slices. Add to the bowl.
3. In a small jug, whisk together the olive oil, vinegar and lemon juice and season with salt and pepper. Just before serving, add the dressing to the bowl and toss everything together to coat.

BLT SALAD

Serves 4–6
Preparation time: 10 minutes
Cooking time: 5 minutes

For the salad
2 slices of white sourdough bread
2 tbsp garlic-infused olive oil
2 little gem (bibb) lettuces,
    washed and shredded
5 medium tomatoes, diced
50g/1¾oz Bacon Bits (see page 15)

For the dressing
2 tbsp extra virgin olive oil
3 tbsp apple cider vinegar
¼ tsp ground black pepper
3 tbsp Vegan Mayonnaise
    (optional – see page 194)

All the flavour of a BLT sandwich in the form of a salad, so you can feel more virtuous eating it. The combination of sweet, juicy tomatoes, crisp lettuce leaves, chewy bread croutons, crunchy, salty bacon and creamy mayo will make your tastebuds tingle.

1. To make the croutons, tear the bread into chunks and fry them in the garlic-infused olive oil over a high heat for 5 minutes.
2. Add all the salad ingredients, including the croutons, to a large bowl and toss to combine.
3. To make the dressing, whisk the olive oil, vinegar and pepper together in a small bowl and drizzle onto the salad. Add a few dollops of mayonnaise, if desired, and serve immediately.

WEEKNIGHT DINNERS

CIDER AND BEAN STEW WITH HERBY DUMPLINGS

Serves 4
Preparation time: 20 minutes
Cooking time: 45 minutes

A generous serving of cider adds a deliciously sharp sweetness to this hearty, comforting stew. The dumplings couldn't be easier to make and create a wonderfully soft, melt-in-your-mouth topping.

For the stew
1 tbsp olive oil
1 white onion, diced
3 garlic cloves, finely chopped
1 leek, sliced
2 carrots, peeled and cut into chunks
1 tsp dried mixed herbs
1 tbsp tomato purée (paste)
1 x 400g/14oz can of butter beans,
    drained and rinsed
1 x 400g/14oz can of flageolet
    beans, drained and rinsed
250ml/9fl oz (1 cup) dry (hard) cider
200ml/7fl oz (scant 1 cup) vegetable stock
1 large handful kale, washed
    and roughly chopped
sea salt and ground black pepper

For the dumplings
130g/4½oz (1 cup) self-raising
    (self-rising) flour
1 tsp dried mixed herbs
1 tbsp English mustard
75g/2½oz (5 tbsp) vegetable shortening

1. Heat the oil in a large oven-safe casserole dish over a medium heat and fry the onion, garlic, leek and carrots for 5 minutes until softening.
2. Stir in the herbs, tomato purée, both types of beans, the cider and stock. Simmer for 15 minutes, then stir in the kale and simmer for a further 5 minutes. Meanwhile, preheat the oven to 150°C fan/170°C/325°F/gas 3.
3. Prepare the dumplings by adding all the ingredients to a small bowl and whisking with a fork until it starts to become dough-like. Once it is coming together, use your hands to knead it and roll it into a long sausage shape. Use a sharp knife to cut the dough into 12 equal pieces. Roll the pieces into balls.
4. Turn off the hob and place the dumplings on top of the stew. Transfer the pan to the oven and cook, uncovered, for another 20 minutes until the dumplings are lightly golden and the liquid has reduced slightly. Season to taste and serve.

STICKY SAUSAGE AND POTATO TRAYBAKE

Serves 2–4
Preparation time: 15 minutes
Cooking time: 40 minutes

2 tbsp vegetable oil
700g/1lb 9oz medium
    potatoes, peeled and cut
    into medium chunks
2 medium carrots, peeled
    and chopped into
    2.5cm/1in pieces
1 red onion, roughly chopped
3 garlic cloves, crushed
8 Vegan Sausages (see page 63)
2 tbsp onion chutney
1 tsp golden syrup (light
    corn syrup)
3 sprigs of fresh thyme
sea salt and ground
    black pepper
Gravy of choice (see
    page 84), to serve

An easy one-pot weeknight dinner that makes use of any vegetables you need to use up in the fridge. One of my favourite variations is to add paprika and use red peppers instead of carrot, then serve with chickpeas.

1. Preheat the oven to 180°C fan/200°C/400°F/gas 6. Add the oil to a large roasting tray and put it in the oven to heat up.
2. Put the potatoes in a large saucepan and cover with cold water. Bring to the boil and par-boil for 5 minutes. Drain well.
3. Add the potatoes to the hot tray, along with the carrots, onion and garlic. Roast for 20 minutes. Remove from the oven and add the sausages, chutney, syrup and thyme, mix everything together and return to the oven for 10–15 minutes.
4. Season with salt and pepper and serve with gravy.

VEGGIE MINCE

Serves 4
Preparation time: 10 minutes

125g/4½oz (heaped 1 cup) walnuts
250g/9oz shiitake or chestnut (cremini)
    mushrooms, roughly chopped
1 tbsp plain (all-purpose) flour
    (gluten-free, if needed)
1 tbsp balsamic vinegar
1 tsp yeast extract or miso paste
a pinch of ground black pepper

Soy mince is easy to find in any supermarket now, but here is a homemade soy-free mince for allergy sufferers or those looking for an alternative option.

1. Put the walnuts in a food processor and pulse until chopped. Add the rest of the ingredients and pulse until you have a chunky mixture. If you don't have a food processor, finely chop the mushrooms and bash the walnuts, wrapped in a clean towel, with a rolling pin, until crushed, then mix with the rest of the ingredients.
2. Use in place of ordinary mince in a variety of dishes such as Shepherd's Pie (see page 60) and Spag Bol (see page 66). Cooks in 10 minutes.

SHEPHERD'S PIE WITH CHAMP MASH

Serves 4
Preparation time: 20 minutes
Cooking time: 1 hour

1 tbsp olive oil
1 large onion, diced
2 carrots, peeled and diced
1 celery stick, diced
3 garlic cloves, crushed
1 tsp yeast extract
2 tbsp tomato purée (paste)
1 tsp dried mixed herbs
1 recipe quantity of Veggie Mince (see page
    59) or 500g/1lb 2oz frozen soy mince
2 tbsp plain (all-purpose) flour
250ml/9fl oz (1 cup) vegetable stock
sea salt and ground black pepper

For the mash

1kg/2lb 4oz King Edward potatoes,
    peeled and diced
75g/2½oz (5 tbsp) dairy-free butter
3 spring onions (scallions), sliced
4–6 tbsp unsweetened almond milk
3 handfuls of grated vegan mozzarella or
    2 tbsp nutritional yeast (optional)

If, like me, you're tired of vegan shepherd's pies that disappoint you, then I promise this recipe will deliver on a more classic, authentic flavour. A meaty, rich filling topped with the fluffiest, most buttery spring onion mash. Once you try it with champ, you won't go back to ordinary mash.

1. Preheat the oven to 180°C fan/200°C/400°F/gas 6. Put the potatoes in a large saucepan and cover with cold water. Bring to the boil and cook for about 20 minutes until the potatoes are soft.
2. Meanwhile, heat the oil in a large frying pan and fry the onion, carrots, celery and garlic over a medium heat for 5 minutes, until soft. Stir in the yeast extract, tomato purée and herbs and cook for a further couple of minutes.
3. Add the veggie mince and flour, stir well to make sure the flour has been absorbed, then add the vegetable stock and simmer for 10 minutes. Taste and season with salt and pepper. Transfer the filling to an oven dish, then prepare the mash.
4. Drain the potatoes and leave to steam in the colander for a minute or two. Add the butter and spring onions to the same hot pan and cook for a couple of minutes before adding the potatoes back in, along with a splash of milk (add it in a bit at a time, adding more if needed), the cheese, if using. Mash everything together until smooth then season to taste.
5. Spread the mash on top of the filling in the dish and use the back of a spoon or a fork to create ridges on top of the mash. Cook for 30 minutes until golden brown on top.

BANGERS AND MASH

Serves 4
Preparation time: 20 minutes
Cooking time: 25 minutes

For the mash
900g/2lb King Edward potatoes,
    peeled and diced
50g/1¾oz (3½ tbsp) dairy-free butter
100ml/3½fl oz (scant ½ cup)
    unsweetened dairy-free milk

For the vegan sausages
2 tbsp vegetable oil
1 small white onion,
    roughly chopped
2 garlic cloves, finely chopped
1 tbsp balsamic vinegar
1 tbsp yeast extract or miso paste
100g/3½oz shiitake or chestnut
    (cremini) mushrooms, sliced
1 x 400g/14oz can of kidney
    beans, drained and rinsed
25g/1oz (¼ cup) chopped walnuts
50g/1¾oz (⅓ cup) porridge
    oats (oatmeal)
2 tbsp plain (all-purpose) flour
1 tsp dried sage
2 tsp tomato purée (paste)
sea salt and ground black pepper
Gravy of choice (see page
    84), to serve

Vegan sausages are not hard to find these days but sometimes it's nice to make your own, especially if you have some mushrooms to use up. Serve with a mash that is just as creamy, buttery and comforting as the dairy-laden kind.

1. Put the potatoes in a large saucepan and cover with cold water. Bring to the boil and cook for 20 minutes, or until very soft.
2. Meanwhile, heat 1 tablespoon of the oil in a frying pan and sauté the onion and garlic for 5 minutes, until softened. Add the balsamic vinegar, yeast extract or miso paste and mushrooms then cook for a further 8 minutes until everything is brown and sticky. Remove from the heat and allow to cool for 10 minutes.
3. Add the mushroom mixture to a food processor along with the beans, walnuts, oats, flour, sage and tomato purée then season to taste. Pulse until you have a smooth, meaty mixture. Shape the mixture into 8 sausages.
4. Add the rest of the oil to a frying pan over a medium heat and cook the sausages for 10 minutes, turning regularly to cook evenly.
5. Once the potatoes are very soft, drain and return them to the pan, along with the butter and milk. Mash until smooth and season.
6. Serve a generous few dollops of mash onto each plate and top with two sausages and some gravy.

LANCASHIRE HOTPOT

Serves 4
Preparation time: 25 minutes, plus marinating
Cooking time: 1 hour 30 minutes

A centuries-old dish that is still popular today. This hearty meat-free version uses jackfruit and oyster mushrooms in a rich gravy and is topped with crisp layers of potato.

1 x 400g/14oz can jackfruit,
    drained and rinsed well
200g/7oz oyster mushrooms
2 tbsp vegetable oil
2 tsp yeast extract or miso paste
2 tbsp balsamic vinegar
1 large onion, finely sliced
1 carrot, peeled and diced
1 tsp dried mixed herbs
2 tbsp plain (all-purpose) flour
500ml/17fl oz/2 cups
    low-salt vegetable stock
750g/1lb 10oz King Edward potatoes,
    peeled and sliced into thin discs
2 tbsp dairy-free butter, melted
a few sprigs of fresh thyme
sea salt and ground black pepper

1. Break the jackfruit into pieces with your hands and put in a large bowl. Use two forks to tear shreds from the mushrooms and add to the bowl. Top with 1 tablespoon of the oil, the yeast extract or miso paste and balsamic vinegar and mix everything together until it is well coated. Allow to marinate for at least an hour, or overnight.
2. Preheat the oven to 150°C fan/170°C/325°F/gas 3. Add the remaining 1 tablespoon of oil to a wide, shallow oven-safe casserole dish and fry the onion and carrot for 5 minutes over a medium heat, until softened. Add
the marinated jackfruit mixture and the dried herbs. Cook for a further 5 minutes.
3. Stir in the flour until fully incorporated, then pour the stock into the pan. Bring to the boil, then reduce the heat and simmer for 15 minutes, until you have a rich, dark gravy.
4. Top the stew with concentric circles of sliced potatoes, working your way from the outside into the centre, overlapping each slice. Brush with the melted butter, put the lid on and cook in the oven for 40 minutes.
5. Remove the lid from the pan, increase the temperature to 180°C fan/200°C/400F/gas 6 and cook for a further 20 minutes, until the potatoes are golden and crisp on top. Sprinkle some fresh thyme over the hotpot during the last 5 minutes of cooking.

SPAG BOL

Serves 6
Preparation time: 10 minutes
Cooking time: 1 hour 15 minutes

1 tbsp olive oil
1 large onion, diced
1 medium carrot, peeled and diced
1 celery stick, diced
3 garlic cloves, crushed
1 tbsp balsamic vinegar
1 tsp yeast extract or miso paste
200g/7oz chestnut (cremini)
    mushrooms, sliced
500g/1lb 2oz frozen soy mince or 1 recipe
    quantity of Veggie Mince (see page 59)
2 x 400g/14oz tins plum tomatoes
150ml/5fl oz (scant ⅔ cup) vegetable stock
6 fresh basil leaves, finely chopped
1 tsp dried oregano
1 tbsp tomato ketchup
8–10 fresh cherry tomatoes, halved
400g/14oz dried spaghetti
sea salt and ground black pepper
vegan Parmesan or nutritional
    yeast, to serve (optional)

Not strictly British, obviously, but one of the nation's favourite dinners so I had to include it. This makes up a big batch that can be frozen or served throughout the week (and it tastes better after a day or two anyway).

1. Add the oil to a large saucepan over a medium heat and sauté the onion, carrot, celery and garlic for 5 minutes, until softened. Stir in the balsamic vinegar, yeast extract or miso paste, mushrooms and mince. Cook for a further 10 minutes.
2. Pour in the tinned tomatoes, vegetable stock, herbs, ketchup and cherry tomatoes. Bring to a boil, then reduce to a simmer and put the lid on the pan. Cook for 1 hour, stirring occasionally, until thick and rich. Season to taste with salt and pepper.
3. Cook the spaghetti according to packet instructions. Serve a ladle of the bolognese on top of the spaghetti, along with a generous grating of Parmesan or nutritional yeast.

TOFU KORMA

Serves 4
Preparation time: 15 minutes
Cooking time: 25 minutes

For the sauce
1 tbsp coconut oil
1 onion, roughly chopped
a thumb-sized piece of ginger,
    peeled and roughly chopped
3 garlic cloves, smashed
1 red chilli, deseeded and
    roughly chopped
2 tsp medium curry powder
a pinch of sea salt
2 tbsp tomato purée (paste)
3 tbsp ground almonds
1 x 400ml/14oz can of coconut milk
60ml/2fl oz (¼ cup) vegetable stock

For the curry
1 tbsp coconut oil
1 red (bell) pepper, sliced
350g/12oz tofu, drained and
    cut into 2.5cm/1in cubes
a large handful raw cashews
a large handful of spinach, washed
    and roughly chopped
a handful of fresh coriander
    (cilantro) leaves, roughly
    torn, plus extra to serve
cooked rice, to serve (optional)

A regular weeknight favourite of mine is this creamy, flavourful tofu korma. Great for fridge-clearing as almost any vegetable works well in this curry.

1. Start with the sauce: add the coconut oil to a medium saucepan over a medium heat and sauté the onion, ginger, garlic and chilli for 3 minutes, until softened.
2. Stir in the curry powder, salt, tomato purée, almonds, coconut milk and stock. Bring to a boil, then reduce the heat and simmer for 2 minutes. Add everything to a blender and blitz to a smooth, creamy sauce.
3. To make the curry, melt the coconut oil in a large saucepan. Fry the red pepper and tofu for 5 minutes over a medium heat, until browned. Stir in the sauce and add the cashews. Simmer for 10–15 minutes until the vegetables are tender. Stir in the spinach and coriander during the last minute of cooking so that they are just wilted.
4. Serve the curry with rice or by itself. Top with extra coriander.

BEEFY MUSHROOM STEW WITH CAULIFLOWER MASH

Serves 4–6
Preparation time: 15 minutes
Cooking time: 40 minutes

2 tbsp vegetable oil
1 red onion, thinly sliced
1 carrot, peeled and sliced
3 garlic cloves, crushed
1 tbsp balsamic vinegar
1 tsp yeast extract or miso paste
1 tbsp tomato purée (paste)
300g/10½oz portobello mushrooms,
    roughly chopped
200g/7oz mixed mushrooms,
    such as shiitake or chestnut
    (cremini), sliced
2 tbsp plain (all-purpose) flour
350ml/12fl oz (1½ cups)
    vegetable stock
1 x 390g/13¾oz can of green
    lentils, drained and rinsed
a large handful of baby
    spinach, washed

For the cauliflower mash
1 large head cauliflower,
    broken into florets
2 tbsp dairy-free butter
2 garlic cloves, finely chopped
 a small pinch of ground
    turmeric (optional)
4 tbsp unsweetened dairy-free milk
a small handful of chives, chopped
sea salt and ground black pepper

If you're craving something really satisfying and wholesome, this stew really hits the spot. The cauliflower mash gives a wonderful, lighter feel but feel free to serve with potato mash, if you prefer (see page 63).

1. Add the oil to a large frying pan over a medium heat and sauté the onion, carrot and garlic for 5 minutes, until softened. Add the vinegar, yeast extract or miso paste, tomato purée and mushrooms and cook for 10 minutes.
2. Stir in the flour until fully incorporated, then pour in the vegetable stock. Bring to the boil, then reduce the heat and simmer for a further 15 minutes, until the stew is rich and thick.
3. Stir in the lentils and spinach, allowing the spinach to wilt for a minute in the pan.
4. While the stew is cooking, make the cauliflower mash. Bring a medium saucepan of water to the boil and place a colander on top. Add the cauliflower florets to the colander and put a lid on top. Steam for 10 minutes, or until they are very soft.
5. Drain the pan and add the butter and garlic. Fry over a medium heat for 2 minutes, then stir in the cauliflower. Season with salt and pepper, add the turmeric, if using, and add half of the milk. Mash well with a potato masher, or use a stick blender for a smoother texture, adding more milk if needed. Stir in the chopped chives.
6. To serve, add a generous dollop of the mash to each plate and pour the mushroom stew on top.

HAGGIS WITH NEEPS AND TATTIES

Serves 4–6
Preparation time: 30 minutes
Cooking time: 1
hour 30 minutes

1 tbsp vegetable oil
1 onion, diced
3 garlic cloves, crushed
1 carrot, peeled and grated
3 portobello mushrooms,
    finely chopped
1 tbsp balsamic vinegar
1 tsp yeast extract or
    miso paste
50g/1¾oz (¼ cup) risotto rice
200ml/7fl oz (scant 1 cup)
    vegetable stock
1 x 390g/13¾oz can green
    lentils, drained and rinsed
100g/3½oz (1 cup) porridge
    oats (oatmeal)
50g/1¾oz vegetable suet

To serve
Swede and Carrot Mash
    (see page 82)
Potato Mash (see page 63)
Gravy of choice (see page 84)

I think this recipe would impress those with fond memories of haggis and those with not-so-fond memories of haggis. It captures the essence of the classic dish whilst being a wonderful vegan recipe in its own right. This flavourful loaf, packed with plant-based protein, makes a perfect Burns night dinner, served with the traditional two types of mash.

1. Heat the oil in a large frying pan and fry the onion, garlic and carrot for 3 minutes over a medium heat, until softened. Stir in the mushrooms, vinegar and yeast extract or miso paste and cook for a further 5–7 minutes.
2. Add the rice and stock, bring to the boil, then reduce the heat and simmer gently for 20 minutes, until the rice is cooked and sticky. Stir regularly and add more water, if needed.
3. Stir in the lentils and oats and set aside to cool. Once cooled, stir in the suet.
4. Tip the mixture onto a baking tray lined with greaseproof paper and work into a log shape, adding a drop of water if it is too dry and crumbly. Wrap the haggis with the paper, then add a layer of foil over the top to make it watertight.
5. Put the wrapped haggis log in a saucepan filled with about 2.5cm/1in water. Bring to the boil then reduce to a simmer and cook for 1 hour until firm.
6. Unwrap the haggis and serve with a dollop each of neeps and tatties, plus a drizzle of gravy.

HOMITY PIE

Serves 8
Preparation time: 30 minutes,
plus chilling
Cooking time: 55 minutes

For the pastry
250g/9oz (1¾ cups) plain
   (all-pupose) flour
125g/4½oz (½ cup) dairy-
   free butter
a pinch of sea salt

For the filling
750g/1lb 10oz King Edward
   potatoes, peeled and
   cut into quarters
2 tbsp dairy-free butter, plus
   extra for greasing
1 large white onion, diced
1 leek, sliced
3 garlic cloves, crushed
100g/3½oz baby spinach,
   washed and roughly torn
150g/5½oz vegan Cheddar-
   style cheese, grated
a pinch of ground nutmeg
250ml/9fl oz (1 cup) Cashew
   Cream (see page 189)
sea salt and ground black pepper

Homity Pie became particularly popular in Britain during the 1960s thanks to the hippy sub-culture making vegetarian dishes more mainstream. I've made it extra-hippy by creating my own vegan version – and it is SO good.

1. Make the pastry by putting the flour, butter and salt in a large bowl and rubbing together with your fingertips until it forms a dense, sandy mixture. (Alternatively, use a food processor and pulse a few times.) Add up to 4 tablespoons of cold water, a spoonful at a time, until the dough comes together without crumbling. Wrap in greaseproof paper and leave to chill in the fridge whilst you make the filling.
2. Put the potatoes in a large saucepan and cover with cold water. Bring to the boil and cook for 10 minutes, until tender. Drain and leave in the colander.
3. Meanwhile, add the butter to the same pan and sauté the onion, leek and garlic for 5 minutes, until softened. Add the spinach to the pan and allow to wilt for 1 minute. Add the onion mixture to the pan along with the drained potatoes, half of the cheese and the nutmeg. Season with salt and pepper, to taste, and allow everything to cool.
4. Preheat the oven to 170°C fan/190°C/375°F/gas 5 and grease a 20cm/8in pastry dish with a little butter.
5. Remove the pastry from the fridge and roll into a circle large enough to cover the base and sides of the pastry dish. Line the dish, trim off the excess pastry and pinch around the rim to create a neat edge. Transfer the cooled potato mixture into the pastry case, then slowly pour in the cashew cream and scatter the remaining cheese over the top. Bake for 25 minutes until golden brown on top.
6. Allow to cool slightly before serving. Delicious served hot or cold.

SUNDAY ROAST

EASY LENTIL LOAF

Serves 6
Preparation time: 15 minutes
Cooking time: 55 minutes

1 tbsp vegetable oil
1 small onion, diced
3 garlic cloves, crushed
2 portobello mushrooms,
    finely chopped
1 carrot, peeled and grated
1 x 400g/14oz can kidney
    beans, drained and rinsed
1 x 400g/14oz can Puy lentils,
    drained and rinsed
1 tbsp yeast extract
    or miso paste
2 tbsp dried mixed herbs
4 tbsp nutritional yeast
    (optional)
140g/5oz (scant 1½ cups)
    oats (oatmeal), plus
    extra if needed
sea salt and ground
    black pepper

*This is my go-to for roast dinners. It's really easy
to make, has a wonderfully meaty texture and is a
lovely change from nut roasts.*

1. Preheat the oven to 160°C fan/180°C/350°F/gas 4
   and line a 900g/2lb loaf tin with greaseproof paper.
2. Heat the oil in a large saucepan over a medium heat
   and sauté the onion for 5 minutes until softened. Add
   the garlic and cook for another 2 minutes.
3. Add the rest of the ingredients and use a potato
   masher to mash everything together to make a
   chunky mixture. If the mixture is too dry, add a drop
   of water and if it's too wet, add more oats. Season
   well with salt and pepper
4. Transfer the mixture to the prepared loaf tin and
   cook for 45 minutes, until firm to the touch.
5. Turn the loaf out onto a chopping board and slice
   to serve.

BUTTERY SEASONAL GREENS

Serves 6
Preparation time: 2 minutes
Cooking time: 8 minutes

Don't worry, greens are optional. I happen to love them though, for the flavour, nutritional goodness and colour it adds to the plate.

900g/2lb seasonal cooking greens, such
    as chard, kale or cabbage, washed,
    trimmed and roughly chopped
80g/2¾oz (5½ tbsp) dairy-free butter
sea salt and ground black pepper

1. Bring a large saucepan of water to the boil and blanch the greens for 5 minutes, until tender, then drain.
2. Melt the butter in the still-warm pan, then remove from the heat. Add the drained greens and stir gently to coat them.
3. Season with salt and pepper, then serve.

CRISPY ROAST POTATOES

Serves 6
Preparation time: 5 minutes
Cooking time: 55 minutes

Having the perfect crispy-on-the-outside and fluffy-on-the-inside potatoes is the most important part of a roast dinner, in my opinion. Trying not to eat them all before serving to guests is the trickiest part.

1.5kg/3lb 5oz King Edward potatoes, peeled
sunflower oil, for cooking
2 tbsp semolina
sea salt

1. Preheat the oven to 210°C fan/230°C/450°F/gas 8 and cover the base of a large roasting tray with oil, about 2mm/¹/₁₆in deep. Put the tray in the oven to get really hot.
2. Cut the potatoes into large chunks, with as much surface area as possible. Put into a large saucepan with cold, lightly salted water and bring to the boil, then boil for 5 minutes.
3. Drain the potatoes and leave them to steam in the colander for a few minutes. Return to the pan and put the lid on, then give it a good shake to roughen up the edges and help make them crispier. Sprinkle the potatoes with the semolina and shake again to coat.
4. Carefully remove the tray from the oven and tip in the potatoes, turning with tongs to coat them in the oil. Roast for 50 minutes, turning half way through, until crisp and golden. Season with salt to serve.

GOLDEN ROASTED PARSNIPS AND CARROTS

Serves 6
Preparation time: 10 minutes
Cooking time: 40 minutes

400g/14oz carrots, peeled and
    cut into battons
400g/14oz parsnips, peeled
    and cut into battons
2 tbsp olive oil
2 tbsp golden syrup (light corn syrup)
1 tbsp wholegrain mustard
a few fresh sage leaves, roughly torn
4 sprigs of rosemary
4 sprigs thyme
a pinch of sea salt

Golden syrup might seem like an odd ingredient in your roast dinner but it really brings out the natural sweetness of the parsnips and carrots, without being overpowering.

1. Preheat the oven to 200°C fan/220°C/425°F/gas 7 and place a large roasting tray in the oven.
2. Combine the olive oil, golden syrup, mustard, herbs and salt in a large bowl. Add the vegetables and toss to coat.
3. Transfer the vegetables to the hot roasting tray and cook for 35 minutes until tender and golden.

SWEDE AND CARROT MASH

Serves 6
Preparation time: 10 minutes
Cooking time: 15 minutes

600g/14oz carrots, peeled and
    roughly chopped
600g/14oz swede, peeled and
    roughly chopped
60g/2oz (¼ cup) dairy-free butter
a small pinch of nutmeg
sea salt and ground black pepper

This buttery swede and carrot mash is perfect for soaking up gravy.

1. Bring a large saucepan of water to the boil. Add the carrots and swede and simmer for 15 minutes, until they are very tender.
2. Drain the vegetables and return them to the saucepan, along with the butter and nutmeg, and season to taste. Mash well with a potato masher, or use a stick blender for a smoother mash.

GRAVY – THREE WAYS

Trying out new gravy variations is a great way to add a twist to your traditional Sunday lunch or with Bangers and Mash (see page 63).

Serves 4–6
Preparation time: about 10 minutes
Cooking time: about 30 minutes

CARAMELISED ONION

1 tbsp vegetable oil
2 red onions, thinly sliced
1 tbsp light brown sugar
2 tbsp balsamic vinegar
2 tbsp plain (all-purpose) flour
600ml/21fl oz (generous 2½ cups) vegetable stock

1. Heat the oil in a medium saucepan and fry the onions over a low heat for 15 minutes, until soft and caramelised. Add the sugar and vinegar and cook for a further 5 minutes.
2. Sprinkle the flour into the pan and stir until the flour has been incorporated and made a thick paste. Add the stock and bring to a boil whilst stirring, then lower the heat and simmer for a further 10–15 minutes, until reduced and thickened. Serve immediately.

CREAMY CIDER

1 tsp vegetable oil
1 onion, finely sliced
2 tbsp plain (all-purpose) flour
a few sprigs of fresh thyme
300ml/10½fl oz (1¼ cups) vegetable stock
200ml/7fl oz (scant 1 cup) dry (hard) cider
4 tbsp Cashew Cream (see page 189)

1. Heat the oil in a medium saucepan and fry the onions over a low heat for 10 minutes, until softened and golden.
2. Sprinkle the flour into the pan and stir until the flour has been incorporated and made a thick paste. Add the thyme and stock and bring to a boil, then lower the heat and simmer for 10 minutes.
3. Add the cider and simmer for a further 5 minutes until reduced and thickened. Remove from the heat and stir in the cashew cream whilst still hot. Serve immediately.

MUSHROOM

2 tbsp dairy-free butter
1 onion, finely sliced
500g/1lb 2oz chestnut (cremini) mushrooms, sliced
3 garlic cloves, crushed
1 tbsp balsamic vinegar
1 tbsp soy sauce
2 tbsp plain (all-purpose) flour
600ml/21fl oz (generous 2½ cups) vegetable or mushroom stock

1. Heat the butter in a medium saucepan and fry the onion over a low heat for 2 minutes, until softened. Add the mushrooms, garlic, vinegar and soy sauce and cook for 15 minutes.
2. Sprinkle the flour into the pan and stir until the flour has been incorporated and made a thick paste. Add the stock and bring to a boil, then lower the heat and simmer for a further 10–15 minutes, until reduced and thickened. Serve immediately.

YORKSHIRE PUDDINGS

Makes 10
Preparation time: 10 minutes
Cooking time: 35 minutes

10 tbsp vegetable oil
80g/2¾oz (scant ⅔ cup) self-
    raising (self-rising) flour
½ tsp baking powder
½ tsp xanthan gum
a pinch of sea salt
60g/2oz (⅓ cup) cornflour
    (cornstarch)
60g/2oz (½ cup) gram flour
    (chickpea flour)
200ml/7fl oz (scant 1
    cup) unsweetened
    dairy-free milk
1 tbsp apple cider vinegar

*This is the recipe I have spent by far the longest
perfecting. Finally, I can share some Yorkshire
puddings I am proud of!*

1. Preheat the oven to 230°C fan/250°C/500°F/gas 9
   and pour a tablespoon of oil into each hole of the
   10-hole muffin tray. Once the oven is really hot, put
   the tray in and leave there for 15 minutes.
2. Meanwhile, prepare the batter by mixing all the
   ingredients together in a blender until smooth.
3. Carefully remove the muffin tray from the oven and,
   working quickly as possible, pour the batter into the
   holes using a circular motion to help form a well in
   the centre.
4. Cook for 25–30 minutes until crisp and golden.
   Carefully remove from the tray and serve
   immediately. These can also be frozen in an airtight
   container for up to 3 months.

PUB GRUB

BEER-BATTERED TOFISH AND CHIPS

Not only does this beer-battered tofu look like the real deal but it also has added fish flavour, thanks to the nori sheet. Served with probably the best chips you'll ever make – which take a bit of effort but are totally worth it – and super-simple minted mushy peas.

Serves 2
Preparation time:
20 minutes, plus cooling
Cooking time: 30 minutes

For the tofish
1 x 390g/13¾oz block of extra firm
   tofu, drained and patted dry
1 sheet of nori
juice of 1 lemon
80g/2¾oz (scant ⅔ cup) plain
   (all-purpose) flour
50g/1¾oz (½ cup) cornflour (cornstarch)
150ml/5fl oz (scant ⅔ cup)
   vegan-friendly pale ale

For the chips
1kg/2lb 4oz King Edward potatoes,
   peeled and cut into chunky chips
750ml/26fl oz (3¼ cups)
   vegetable oil, for frying

For the mushy peas
1 tbsp dairy-free butter
200g/7oz (1½ cups) frozen petit pois
a handful of fresh mint leaves,
   finely chopped
1 tsp white (distilled) vinegar
sea salt and ground black pepper

To serve
vinegar
Vegan Mayonnaise (see page 194)
1 lemon, cut into wedges

1. Rinse the chips in cold water to remove excess starch. Add them to a large saucepan of cold, salted water and bring to the boil, then lower the heat and simmer for 5–8 minutes until just softened. Drain, pat dry and arrange on a baking tray. Refrigerate for at least an hour or, covered, overnight.
2. Make the mushy peas. Melt the butter in a small saucepan over a medium heat. Add the peas and cook for 5 minutes until soft. Add the mint and vinegar and, using a potato masher, crush the peas until mushy. Season then place a lid on the pan to keep them warm.
3. To cook the chips, heat the oil to approximately 180°C/350°F and carefully lower half of the potatoes into the oil. Cook for 4–5 minutes, or until they are crisp and golden. Use a slotted spoon to carefully remove the chips from the oil and drain on some paper towel. Repeat with the remaining potatoes. Season generously with salt.
4. Whilst the chips are cooking, prepare the tofish. Cut the block in half horizontally, then create fillet shapes, triangles or just rectangles. Using scissors, cut the nori sheet into matching shapes, so that it sits neatly on top of the tofu. This will resemble fish skin and also adds a fish flavour. Squeeze half a lemon over the tofu pieces then pat the nori shapes on top, so they're fairly secure.
5. Use the same pot of oil as you used to fry the chips, and reheat it until it's reached approximately 160°C/315°F. Make the batter by whisking together the flour, cornflour and ale, then season. Dip the tofu shapes into the batter and then carefully transfer them to the hot oil. Cook for 3–4 minutes, or until golden brown. Remove from the oil with a slotted spoon.
6. Sprinkle the tofish with salt and vinegar and serve with the chips, peas, lemon wedges and mayonnaise.

These are some of my favourite homemade snacks. They can also be made into bite-sized portions to be served at parties. Delicious both hot and cold!

SAUSAGE ROLLS

Makes: 8
Preparation time: 15 minutes
Cooking time: 25 minutes

2 x 320g/11¼oz sheets of
    vegan puff pastry
8 Vegan Sausages (see page 63)
aquafaba or unsweetened
    dairy-free milk, for brushing

1. Preheat the oven to 160°C fan/180°C/350°F/gas 4 and line a baking tray with greaseproof paper.
2. Unroll the pastry sheets and cut both into quarters. Place one sausage onto each quarter. Roll up each sausage in its pastry sheet, folding in the ends so it is encased on all sides. Use a sharp knife to make small horizontal cuts along the top of the rolls, then brush them with some aquafaba or milk.
3. Place the rolls on the prepared baking tray and bake for 25 minutes until puffed and golden. Serve hot or cold.

CURRIED VEGGIE PASTIES

Makes 8
Preparation time: 15 minutes
Cooking time: 30 minutes

1 tbsp coconut oil
1 onion, diced
150g/5½oz Veggie Mince (see
    page 59) or shop-bought
100g/3½oz white potatoes,
    peeled and diced
    into small pieces
50g/1¾oz (scant ⅓ cup)
    frozen peas
2 tbsp curry paste
1 tbsp mango chutney
2 x 320g/11¼oz sheets of
    Shortcrust Pastry (see
    page 196) or shop-bought
aquafaba or unsweetened
    dairy-free milk, for brushing

1. Heat the oil in a frying pan and fry the onion, mince and potato for 5 minutes over a medium heat, until the mince has browned. Stir in the peas, curry paste and chutney and cook for a further 3 minutes. Remove from the heat and allow to cool.
2. Preheat the oven to 160°C fan/180°C/350°F/gas 4 and line a large baking tray with greaseproof paper.
3. Unroll the pastry sheets and use an 18cm/7in diameter template to cut out 8 circles, using a small, sharp knife. Brush the edges of the circles with a little aquafaba or milk. Place 3 tablespoons of the filling mixture into the centre of one half of a pastry circle. Fold the empty half of the pastry over the top to create a half-moon shape and use a fork to crimp and seal the edges. Repeat to fill the remaining 7 pasties.
4. Place the pasties on the prepared baking tray and brush with extra aquafaba or milk. Cook for 20 minutes, turning the pasties over halfway through. Serve warm.

ARTICHOKE FISHCAKES WITH DILL MAYO

Makes 12
Preparation time: 15 minutes
Cooking time: 20 minutes

You won't believe how convincing these fishcakes are – in appearance, texture and taste. Delicious served with a salad for a light lunch.

1 x 400g/14oz can of chickpeas,
    drained and liquid
    (aquafaba) reserved
1 x 390g/13¾oz can of artichoke
    hearts, drained and rinsed
180g/6¼oz (scant 4 cups)
    fresh breadcrumbs
2 spring onions (scallions),
    roughly chopped
4 tbsp Vegan Mayonnaise
    (see page 194)
1 tsp mustard
1 tsp dried kelp granules or
    other seaweed (optional)
1 tbsp dried mixed herbs
vegetable oil, for frying
sea salt and ground black pepper

For the dill mayo

a few sprigs of fresh dill, chopped
4 tbsp Vegan Mayonnaise
    (see page 194)
1 lemon, sliced into
    wedges, to serve

1. Add the chickpeas, artichokes, 80g/2¾oz (1½ cups) of the breadcrumbs, spring onions, mayonnaise, mustard, seaweed and mixed herbs to a food processor. Season with a generous pinch of salt and pepper and pulse until everything is chopped and chunky but not smooth. (You can also do this by hand with a potato masher.)
2. Divide the mixture into 12 equal portions and shape into patties. Set aside on a large plate or baking tray.
3. Put the remaining breadcrumbs into a shallow bowl and the reserved aquafaba (this will act as an egg substitute) into another bowl. Dip a patty into the aquafaba and then place in the breadcrumb bowl and press in the crumbs until well coated. Return to the plate or baking tray and repeat to coat all the patties.
4. Meanwhile, put a large frying pan over a high heat and cover the base of the pan with the oill. After a few minutes, use one of the patties to test if the oil is hot enough. If it sizzles and bubbles when added to the pan it's ready. Add half the cakes to the pan and cook for 4–5 minutes on each side until crisp and golden, then transfer to a plate with some paper towel, to absorb any excess oil. Repeat to cook the next batch.
5. Stir the dill into the mayonnaise. Serve the fishcakes with a small bowl of the dill mayo along with some lemon wedges for squeezing.

PORTOBELLO STEAK 'N' KIDNEY BEAN PIE

Serves 4
Preparation time: 20 minutes
Cooking time: 55 minutes

A vegan version of the British classic steak and kidney pie that definitely will not disappoint. This is one of my favourite recipes to win over meat-eaters.

1 tbsp vegetable oil
1 red onion, thinly sliced
3 garlic cloves, crushed
1 tbsp balsamic vinegar
1 tsp yeast extract or
    miso paste
1 tbsp tomato purée (paste)
300g/10½oz portobello
    mushrooms, chopped
    into thick chunks
200g/7oz mixed mushrooms,
    such as shiitake or
    chestnut (cremini), sliced
2 tbsp plain (all-purpose) flour
350ml/12fl oz (1½ cups)
    vegetable stock
1 x 400g/14oz can kidney
    beans, drained and rinsed
2 x 320g/11¼oz sheets of
    vegan puff pastry
aquafaba or unsweetened
    dairy-free milk, for brushing

1. Heat the oil in a large saucepan and sauté the onion and garlic for 5 minutes, until softened. Add the balsamic vinegar, yeast extract or miso paste, tomato purée and mushrooms and cook for a further 8 minutes.
2. Sprinkle the flour on top and stir to incorporate. Add the stock and bring to a boil, then reduce the heat and simmer for about 5 minutes until you have a gravy-like mixture. Remove from the heat, stir in the beans and allow to cool completely.
3. Preheat the oven to 200°C fan/220°C/425°F/gas 7.
4. Divide the filling into four individual pie dishes. Brush the edges of the dishes with a little aquafaba or milk.
5. Slice both pastry sheets in half and use a half to top each pie dish, crimping the edges to seal and scoring the tops with a sharp knife. Brush the tops with some more aquafaba or milk and bake for 30 minutes, until puffed and golden on top. Serve immediately.

BRITISH VEGGIE BURGER

Serves 2–4

Preparation time: 15 minutes

Cooking time: 25 minutes

1 tbsp vegetable oil, plus extra
    for cooking the burgers

1 onion, finely diced

2 garlic cloves, crushed

1 tbsp balsamic vinegar

1 tsp yeast extract or miso paste

120g/4¼oz shiitake or chestnut (cremini)
    mushrooms, finely chopped

1 tsp dried mixed herbs

1 tbsp brown sauce

½ tsp mustard powder

1 x 400g/14oz can kidney beans,
    drained and rinsed

125g/4½oz (1 cup) cooked rice

40g/1½oz (⅓ cup) porridge oats (oatmeal)

4–6 tbsp plain (all-purpose) flour

a generous pinch of sea salt and
    ground black pepper

To serve

2–4 vegan cheese slices

2–4 seeded burger buns

1 little gem (bibb) lettuce, leaves
    separated and washed

1 beef tomato, sliced

Vegan Mayonnaise (see page 194)

ketchup

Crispy Bacon Strips (see page 15)

This veggie burger has a great, firm texture – no mushiness! It's packed full of flavour and cooks beautifully in the pan, the oven or even on the grill. The recipe makes four small patties or two large ones if you're feeling hungry!

1. Heat the oil in a large pan and sauté the onion and garlic for 5 minutes, until softened. Add the balsamic vinegar, yeast extract or miso paste and mushrooms and cook for a further 8 minutes until brown and sticky.

2. Add all the remaining ingredients and use a potato masher to crush and combine everything together into a thick, chunky mixture. (You can also pulse the mixture in a food processor.) Shape the mixture into two large or four small patties.

3. To cook, heat a frying pan with enough oil to cover the base and fry over a medium heat for 5 minutes on each side, until slightly charred. Add the slices of cheese to the burgers whilst they are still warm in the pan and let the cheese melt slightly.

4. To serve, lay out the bases of the buns and place a cheesy burger on each. Top with lettuce, tomato, mayonnaise, ketchup, bacon slices and any other toppings you like, then pop the bun lid on top and enjoy.

PORKIE PIES

Makes 8
Preparation time: 20 minutes,
plus cooling
Cooking time: 45 minutes,
plus cooling and setting

For the filling
1 tbsp vegetable oil, plus
    extra for greasing
1 small onion, roughly chopped
2 garlic cloves, finely chopped
1 tbsp balsamic vinegar
1 tbsp yeast extract
    or miso paste
100g/3½oz shiitake or chestnut
    (cremini) mushrooms, sliced
1 x 400g/14oz can of red kidney
    beans, drained and rinsed
25g/1oz (heaped ¼ cup)
    chopped walnuts
50g/1¾ oz (½ cup) porridge
    oats (oatmeal)
2 tbsp plain (all-purpose) flour
½ tsp dried mixed herbs
2 tsp tomato purée (paste)
sea salt and ground black pepper

For the pastry
1 recipe quantity Hot Water
    Crust Pastry (see page 195)
aquafaba or unsweetened
    dairy-free milk, for glazing

For the jelly filling
1 tsp vegan gelatine powder
    (such as VegeGel
    or agar agar)
100ml/3½fl oz (scant
    ½ cup) vegetable stock

The pork pie is one of the most famous staples in British cuisine. Perfect as a quick snack, at a picnic or as part of a ploughman's lunch.

1. Heat the oil in a medium saucepan and sauté the onion and garlic for 5 minutes, until softened. Add the balsamic vinegar, yeast extract or miso paste and mushrooms and cook for a further 8 minutes until brown and sticky. Remove from the heat and allow to cool for 10 minutes.
2. Add the mushroom mixture to a food processor along with the beans, walnuts, oats, flour, herbs, tomato purée and salt and pepper, to taste. Pulse until you have a uniformly chunky mixture.
3. Preheat the oven to 160°C fan/180°C/350°F/gas 4. Brush six holes of a muffin tin with some oil.
4. Roll out your pastry on a floured surface to ½cm/¼in thick. Using a small upside-down bowl, cut out circles that are about 2.5cm/1in bigger than the muffin tin holes.
5. Gently press the circles into the greased muffin tin holes to create a neat shape. Don't trim off any extra pastry, but brush the top edge with a little of the aquafaba or milk.
6. Roll the porkie mixture into six even balls then press a ball into each pastry case.
7. Cut smaller circles, roughly the same size as the muffin tin holes, with the remaining pastry. Make a hole in the middle of each them, big enough to fit a funnel nozzle through. Gently place these over the pies and press down the edges with a fork. Use a small sharp knife to trim off the excess pastry around the edges.
8. Brush with the aquafaba or milk and bake for 25 minutes until golden brown. Allow to cool completely.
9. To make the jelly filling, simply whisk the vegetable gelatine powder with the vegetable stock in a small saucepan over a high heat. Bring to a boil then remove from the heat. Pour the liquid through a funnel into the pie holes very slowly until it's just about to overflow. Allow to set for at least 30 minutes. Store the pies in an airtight container in the fridge for up to 3 days.

WELSH RAREBIT

Serves 2
Preparation time: 10 minutes,
plus soaking
Cooking time: 10 minutes

35g/1¼oz (¼ cup) cashew nuts
1 tsp apple cider vinegar
½ tsp sugar
2 tbsp nutritional yeast
2 tbsp arrowroot powder
½ tsp yeast extract, plus extra
    to drizzle (optional)
½ tsp English mustard
¼ tsp onion granules
a small pinch of ground nutmeg
a pinch of sea salt and ground black pepper
1 tbsp olive oil
60ml/2fl oz (¼ cup) stout
60ml/2fl oz (¼ cup) unsweetened
    dairy-free milk
4 slices bread

If you're yet to find the perfect vegan cheese-on-toast substitute, may I present this cheesy, gooey, stretchy Welsh rarebit? It is cashew-based, which results in a rich flavour and texture. This cheese is also amazing for pizzas and toasties.

1. Soak the cashews in 100ml/3½fl oz (scant ½ cup) of just boiled water for at least 15 minutes.
2. Meanwhile, add the rest of the cheese ingredients to a high-powered blender. Tip in the cashews, along with the water they have been soaking in, and blend until smooth.
3. Pour the mixture into a small saucepan over a high heat. Cook, stirring constantly, for 2–3 minutes, or until very thick and stretchy.
4. Preheat the grill (broiler) to high and lightly toast the bread on both sides. Divide the cheesy mixture between the slices and spread over generously. Drizzle on some extra yeast extract, if you like. Grill (broil) for 3–5 minutes or until golden brown and bubbling.

AFTERNOON TEA

SCONES WITH CLOTTED CREAM

Makes 16
Preparation time: 10 minutes
Cooking time: 12 minutes

475g/1lb 1oz (3½ cups) self-raising (self-
rising) flour, plus extra for dusting
50g/1¾oz (¼ cup) caster sugar
85g/3oz (⅓ cup) dairy-free butter
1 tbsp apple cider vinegar
240ml/8fl oz (1 cup) dairy-free milk
a large handful of dried fruit (optional)
aquafaba or dairy-free milk, for brushing
jam, to serve (optional)

For the clotted cream
45g/1½oz (3 tbsp) dairy-free butter
5 tbsp coconut cream (from the top of
a can of chilled coconut milk)
2 tbsp icing (confectioner's) sugar

The perfect, crumbly scone is the pinnacle of afternoon tea, as well as being my favourite thing to bake and eat. Have them plain, with fruit or other flavourings and serve with some jam and homemade vegan clotted cream.

1. Preheat the oven to 180°C fan/200°C/400°F/gas 6 and line a baking tray with greaseproof paper.
2. In a large mixing bowl, combine the flour and sugar. Add the butter a teaspoon at a time and rub into the flour with your fingertips.
3. Once you have a dense, sandy mixture, make a well in the middle. Mix the vinegar with the milk in a small jug and start slowly adding to the bowl, mixing with a wooden spoon until it forms a dough.
4. Turn onto a lightly floured surface and knead briefly until smooth. Add the dried fruit at this point, if using. Flatten the dough into a 1cm/½in thick sheet and cut out the scones using a round 6cm/2½in pastry cutter or upside-down glass. Transfer the scones to the prepared baking tray and brush the tops lightly with some aquafaba or milk.
5. Bake the scones for 10–12 minutes until well-risen and lightly golden.
6. While the scones are baking, make the clotted cream. Whisk the ingredients together for 5 minutes until light and fluffy. Keep refrigerated until just before serving.
7. Serve the scones warm from the oven with jam, or serve cold later on. Store in an airtight container for up to 2 days.

CHEESE SCONES

Makes 16
Preparation time: 10 minutes
Cooking time: 12 minutes

475g/1lb 1oz (3½ cups) self-
    raising (rising) flour
2 tbsp nutritional yeast
1 tbsp dried mixed herbs
120g/4¼oz vegan strong Cheddar-
    style cheese, grated
85g/3oz (⅓ cup) dairy-free butter
240ml/8fl oz (1 cup) dairy-free
    unsweetened milk
1 tbsp apple cider vinegar
6 sundried tomatoes, chopped into
    small chunks (optional)
aquafaba or dairy-free milk, for brushing

*For a savoury afternoon tea treat, you can't beat
a cheese scone. I love adding some herbs and
sundried tomatoes for extra flavour. Wonderful served
with dairy-free butter or vegan cream cheese.*

1. Preheat the oven to 180°C fan/200°C/400°F/gas 6
    and line a baking tray with greaseproof paper.
2. In a large mixing bowl, combine the flour, nutritional
    yeast, mixed herbs and grated cheese. Add the butter
    a teaspoon at a time and rub into the flour with
    your fingertips.
3. Once you have a dense, sandy mixture, make a well in
    the middle. Mix the vinegar with the milk in a small
    jug and start slowly adding to the bowl, mixing with a
    wooden spoon until it forms a dough.
4. Turn onto a lightly floured surface and knead briefly
    until smooth. Add sundried tomatoes at this point, if
    using. Flatten the dough into a 1cm/½in thick sheet
    and cut out the scones using a round 6cm/2½in pastry
    cutter or upside-down glass. Transfer the scones to the
    prepared baking tray and brush the tops lightly with
    some aquafaba or milk.
5. Bake for 10–12 minutes until well-risen and lightly golden.
6. Serve the scones warm from the oven, or serve
    cold later on. Store in an airtight container for up
    to 2 days.

FINGER SANDWICHES

The great thing about these dainty little sandwiches is that they instantly give a fancy tea party vibe but are so ridiculously simple to put together. The filling options are endless but I've included three of my favourites, which work well on both white and wholemeal bread.

CLASSIC CUCUMBER

6 medium slices of soft white bread
dairy-free butter or hummus, for spreading
½ cucumber, cut into very thin slices
a generous pinch of sea salt
¼ tsp white pepper

CORONATION CHICKPEA

6 medium slices of soft white bread
dairy-free butter, for spreading
½ recipe quantity Coronation
      Chickpea Salad (see page 44)

ROASTED RED PEPPER AND PESTO

6 medium slices of soft brown bread
dairy-free butter, for spreading
3–6 tbsp vegan pesto
1 x 290g/10¼oz jar of roasted red peppers,
      drained and sliced into strips
sea salt and ground black pepper

Makes 36
Preparation time: 25 minutes

1. Butter each slice of bread, then add your fillings.
2. For the cucumber, first put the slices in a colander or sieve and sprinkle with the salt. Leave for approximately 15 minutes. Lay out a few pieces of kitchen paper and place the cucumber slices on top to absorb the excess moisture. Gently pat dry and arrange the cucumber slices on one half of the bread, slightly overlapping and season.
3. For the coronation chickpea, simply add a dollop to one half of the bread slices.
4. For the red pepper and pesto, spread 1–2 tablespoons of pesto onto half of the slices. Arrange the chopped peppers onto the remaining slices and season.
5. Bring the sandwich halves together and press down firmly. Carefully remove the crusts and cut into neat finger sandwiches or triangles. Serve immediately.

JAM TARTS

Makes 24
Preparation time: 20 minutes,
plus chilling
Cooking time: 15 minutes

140g/5oz (scant ⅔ cup) dairy-free
    butter, plus extra for greasing
250g/9oz (1¾ cups) plain (all-purpose) flour
1 tbsp cornflour (cornstarch)
30g/1oz (2½ tbsp) caster sugar
a small pinch of sea salt
jams and/or marmalades of choice

This is a fun, easy recipe that both adults and kids will love baking. You can even use ready-made shortcrust pastry to make it extra simple. I love using a variety of different jams and marmalades to mix and match.

1. Preheat the oven to 160°C fan/180°C/350°F/gas 4 and grease two 12-hole shallow bun tins with butter.
2. In a large bowl, stir together the flour, cornflour, sugar and salt. Add the butter and rub it into the flour with your fingertips until well incorporated.
3. Add a couple of tablespoons of cold water and bring the mixture together with a wooden spoon and then your hands until you have a firm dough that holds its shape without crumbling. Wrap in greaseproof paper and chill for 30 minutes.
4. Roll the pastry out to 3mm/⅛in thick and, using a fluted pastry cutter that is slightly bigger than the holes in the tins, cut out the pastry cases. Place them gently into the tin and use your fingers to pat down into shape.
5. Fill each pastry case with a generous teaspoon of jam or marmalade and bake for 15 minutes, or until the jam is bubbling and the pastry is light golden brown. Carefully remove from the oven and leave to cool in the tin for a few minutes before transferring to a wire rack to cool completely. Don't be tempted to try these hot from the oven as the jam will be scalding!

SCOTTISH SHORTBREAD

Serves 8
Preparation time: 15 minutes
Cooking time: 50 minutes

220g/7¾oz (scant 1 cup)
    dairy-free butter, plus
    extra for greasing
a small pinch of sea salt
110g/3¾oz (heaped ½
    cup) caster sugar, plus
    extra for dusting
225g/8oz (1¾ cups) plain
    (all-purpose) flour, sifted
100g/3½oz (1 cup) cornflour
    (cornstarch)

You can use this recipe to make traditional petticoat tails, slices or use cookie cutters to make shaped biscuits. This shortbread is buttery, crumbly and melts in your mouth, just like the traditional kind.

1. Preheat the oven to 150°C fan/170°C/325°F/gas 3 and grease a 23cm/9in round tart tin lightly with butter.
2. Cream the butter, salt and sugar together with a wooden spoon or stand mixer until light and fluffy. Stir in the flours and mix until it forms a ball, being careful not to overwork the dough.
3. Press the dough into the tart tin, creating an even layer. Score into 8 slices with a sharp knife and use a skewer to create a dotted pattern in the dough, for decoration. Dust generously with sugar, then bake for 45–50 minutes, until lightly golden.
4. Leave to cool in the tin before slicing and serving.

VICTORIA SPONGE

Serves 12
Preparation time: 15 minutes
Cooking time: 20 minutes

200g/7oz (scant 1 cup) dairy-free butter
300g/10½oz (1½ cups) caster sugar
180g/6¼oz (¾ cup) soy yoghurt
220ml/7½fl oz (scant 1 cup)
    unsweetened dairy-free milk
1 tbsp apple cider vinegar
2 tsp vanilla extract
400g/14oz (3 cups) self-raising
    (self-rising) flour, sifted
1 tsp baking powder

For the filling
200g/7oz (1½ cups) icing (confectioner's)
    sugar, sifted, plus extra for dusting
160g/5¾oz (⅔ cup) dairy-free butter
1 tsp vanilla extract
5 tbsp seedless raspberry jam

A Victoria sponge is my favourite kind of cake and I'm so happy to say that this vegan version is just as good as the ones I used to love as a child. A light, airy sponge with a sweet and creamy filling: my idea of heaven.

1. Preheat the oven to 160°C fan/180°C/350°F/gas 4 and grease and line two 20cm/8in round sandwich tins (shallow cake pans).
2. Beat the butter and sugar together for 3 minutes, preferably with an electric whisk or mixer, until it's light and fluffy.
3. Stir in the yoghurt, milk, vinegar and vanilla, then gently fold in the flour and baking powder.
4. Divide the mixture between the two prepared tins and bake for 20 minutes, or until a skewer inserted into the middle of the cakes comes out clean. Leave to cool in the tins for a few minutes before turning out onto a wire rack to cool completely.
5. Meanwhile, make the buttercream by beating the icing sugar, butter and vanilla together until light and fluffy.
6. Once the cakes are completely cool, assemble by spreading the top of one cake with the buttercream and the other cake with the jam. Sandwich together, inverting one cake so that both fillings are in the middle, then dust the top of the cake with icing sugar.
7. Cut into 12 slices and enjoy.

LEMON DRIZZLE LOAF

Serves 10
Preparation time: 10 minutes
Cooking time: 30 minutes

100ml/3½fl oz (scant ½
    cup) vegetable oil
200g/7oz (1 cup) caster sugar
1 small lemon, juiced
    and zested
200ml/7fl oz (scant 1
    cup) unsweetened
    dairy-free milk
275g/9¾oz (2 cups) self-
    raising (self-rising) flour
1 tsp baking powder

For the lemon syrup
50g/1¾oz (¼ cup) caster sugar
juice of 1 small lemon

For the topping
juice of 1 small lemon
100g/3½oz) icing
    (confectioner's)
    sugar, sifted
zest of 1 small lemon

This is the best way to use up lemons. Sweet, moist and zingy, this cake is always a winner and so easy to rustle up for an afternoon treat.

1. Preheat the oven to 160°C fan/180°C/350°F/gas 4 and line a 900g/2lb loaf tin with greaseproof paper.
2. Mix the oil with the sugar, lemon juice and zest, and milk. Whisk in the flour and baking powder until you have a smooth batter.
3. Pour the batter into the prepared loaf tin and bake for 30 minutes, or until a skewer inserted into the centre of the cake comes out clean.
4. Meanwhile, make the lemon syrup by melting the sugar with the lemon juice over a medium heat, until the sugar is completely dissolved. Once the cake is baked, poke lots of holes in the top with a skewer and brush the surface with the syrup, whilst it's still warm. Leave to cool completely in the tin.
5. Make the icing by simply mixing the lemon juice and icing sugar together until you have a thick but runny mixture. When the cake has cooled, drizzle on top, allowing some icing to drip down the sides. Sprinkle over the lemon zest to decorate. Allow the icing to set before serving.

COFFEE AND WALNUT CAKE

Serves 10
Preparation time: 20 minutes
Cooking time: 20 minutes

5 tbsp instant coffee granules
400g/14oz (3 cups) self-raising
     (self-rising) flour
240g/8½oz (scant 2¼ cups) caster sugar
1 tsp baking powder
400ml/14fl oz (1¾ cups) unsweetened
     dairy-free milk
160ml/5¼fl oz (⅔ cup) vegetable oil
130g/4½oz (1 heaped cup) chopped walnuts
a few walnut halves, for decorating

For the buttercream

160g/5¾oz (⅔ cup) dairy-free butter
200g/7oz icing (confectioner's) sugar, sifted

This bittersweet cake is perfect with a cuppa. I love the slight crunch you get from the chopped walnuts, paired with the soft, velvety coffee buttercream.

1. Make a paste with the coffee granules and 4 tablespoons of boiling water and leave to cool.
2. Preheat the oven to 160°C fan/180°C/350°F/gas 4 and grease two 23cm/9in round cake tins with a circle of greaseproof paper.
3. In a large bowl, mix the flour, sugar and baking powder together. In a large jug, whisk together the milk, oil and all but 1½ tablespoons of the coffee paste (reserve this for the buttercream). Pour the wet ingredients into the bowl and whisk to make a smooth batter. Stir in the chopped walnuts.
4. Evenly divide the mixture between the prepared cake tins and bake for 20 minutes, or until a skewer inserted into the centre of the cakes comes out clean. Leave to cool in the tin for a few minutes before turning out onto a wire rack to cool completely.
5. Meanwhile, make the buttercream by mixing the reserved coffee paste with the butter and icing sugar until light and fluffy.
6. Spread half the buttercream over the top of one of the cakes, then top with the second cake. Spread the remaining buttercream over the top and decorate with the walnut halves.

BAKEWELL TART

Serves 10
Preparation time: 20 minutes,
plus cooling
Cooking time: 50 minutes

1 recipe quantity of Shortcrust
    Pastry (page 196)
4–6 tbsp seedless raspberry jam
170g/6oz (scant ¾ cup)
    dairy-free butter
150g/5½oz (¾ cup) caster sugar
60g/2oz (¼ cup) unsweetened
    soy yoghurt
120ml/4fl oz (½ cup)
    unsweetened dairy-free milk
2 tsp almond extract
4 tbsp cornflour (cornstarch)
40g/1½oz (heaped ¼ cup) self-
    raising (self-rising) flour
150g/5½oz (1½ cups)
    ground almonds
50g/1¾oz (heaped ½ cup)
    flaked (sliced) almonds
icing (confectioner's)
    sugar, for dusting

Fragrant almond paired with sweet, tart raspberry creates one of Britain's favourite teatime treats. Delicious served warm from the oven with some coconut whipped cream or simply cut into slices and dusted with a little icing sugar.

1. Preheat the oven to 170°C fan/190°C/375°F/gas 5.
2. Roll out the shortcrust pastry to 3mm/⅛in thick and large enough to fit a 36 x 12cm/14 x 4½in loose-based tart tin or a 23cm/9in round tin. Line the tin and trim away the excess pastry from the edges.
3. Use a fork to gently poke a few holes into the base of the pastry and cover with a strip of greaseproof paper. Fill the case with baking beans and blind bake for 15 minutes. Remove the beans and paper and bake for a further 5 minutes until golden brown and allow to cool.
4. Once cooled, spread the jam over the base of the tart in an even layer.
5. Make the frangipane by beating the butter and sugar together until light and fluffy. Stir in the yoghurt, milk and almond extract, then fold in the cornflour, self-raising flour and ground almonds. Dollop the batter over the jam and spread into an even layer. Scatter the flaked almonds over the top.
6. Bake for 30 minutes, or until golden brown and firm to the touch. Allow to cool in the tin before carefully removing. Cut into slices and dust with icing sugar to serve.

BATTENBERG

Serves 10
Preparation time: 30 minutes
Cooking time: 30 minutes

Don't worry, Battenberg is actually much easier to make than you'd think. Not only does it taste wonderful, but just looking at this beautiful pink and yellow chequered cake is a pleasure in itself.

130g/4½oz (generous ½ cup) dairy-free butter
200g/7oz (1 cup) caster sugar
120g/4¼oz (½ cup) unsweetened soy yoghurt
150ml/5fl oz (scant ⅔ cup) unsweetened dairy-free milk
2 tsp apple cider vinegar
1 tsp almond extract
260g/9¼oz (2 cups) self-raising (self-rising) flour
½ tsp baking powder
vegan pink food colouring or beetroot juice
3 tbsp marmalade
400g/14oz golden marzipan
icing (confectioner's) sugar, for dusting

1. Preheat the oven to 160°C fan/180°C/350°F/gas 4. Use a double layer of foil to divide a 20cm/8in square cake tin in half. Line both sections with greaseproof paper.
2. Whisk together the butter and sugar until light and fluffy. Stir in the yoghurt, milk, vinegar and almond extract, then fold in the flour and baking powder.
3. Pour half of the batter into one of the halves in the tin. Mix drops of food colouring or beetroot juice into the remaining half of the batter until you get the desired shade of pink, then pour the pink batter into the other half of the tin.
4. Bake for 25 minutes until a skewer inserted into the centre comes out clean. Allow to cool for a few minutes in the tin before turning out onto a wire rack to cool completely.
5. To decorate, gently transfer the cakes onto a chopping board and cut each one in half lengthways, trimming the edges to create straight and even layers.
6. Heat the marmalade in a small saucepan over a low heat until runny. Brush one long side of a pink strip of cake and one side of a yellow one and stick them together. Repeat to stick the other two strips together. Now paint the top of one pair completely with marmalade and place the other pair on top, with pink on top of yellow and vice versa to create a chequerboard pattern.
7. Dust a work surface with a little icing sugar and roll out the marzipan to a rectangle about 20 x 25cm/8 x 10in. Brush the outside of the cake with marmalade. Use a rolling pin to lift the marzipan over the cake and smooth it firmly around the top and sides, joining underneath. Trim away the excess and brush the seam with a little marmalade. Finish by pressing the edges together to create a seam at the bottom.

EARL GREY TEA LOAF

Serves 10
Preparation time: 15 minutes
Cooking time: 1 hour

2 Earl Grey tea bags
250g/9oz (1¾ cups) dried fruit
275g/9¾oz (2 cups) self-
    raising (self-rising) flour
60g/2oz (heaped ¼ cup)
    dark brown sugar
½ tsp baking powder
1 tsp ground mixed spice
    (apple pie spice)
90g/3¼oz (generous ⅓ cup)
    unsweetened soy yoghurt
2 tbsp marmalade (optional)

A slice of rich, fruity tea loaf with a generous spread of dairy-free butter is one of my favourite things to have as an afternoon snack. To ensure a nice juicy cake, you'll need to soak the fruit overnight, so make sure you allow time before you start baking.

1. Pour 300ml/10½fl oz (1¼ cups) of just boiled water into a large bowl and add the tea bags. Stir in the dried fruit and leave overnight to soak.
2. Preheat the oven to 160°C fan/180°C/350°F/gas 4 and grease a 900g/2lb loaf tin, then line with greaseproof paper.
3. In a large bowl, mix together the flour, sugar, baking powder and mixed spice. Stir in the yoghurt and the fruity tea mixture (including the soaking water).
4. Pour the batter into the prepared loaf tin and bake for 1 hour, or until a skewer inserted into the middle of the loaf comes out clean.
5. Allow to cool in the tin for a few minutes before transferring to a wire rack to cool completely. If you want a glazed, sticky finish, heat the marmalade in a small saucepan and brush over the top of the loaf whilst it's still warm.

SWEETS, PUDDINGS & DESSERTS

BREAD AND BUTTER PUDDING

Serves 6
Preparation time: 15 minutes,
plus standing
Cooking time: 35 minutes

An old-fashioned British dessert that never gets old. Turn your leftover stale bread into this delicious, comforting pudding filled with custard, dried fruit and warm spices.

100g/3½oz (7 tbsp) dairy-free butter,
　　plus extra for greasing
10 thick slices day-old white crusty
　　bread, crusts removed
80g/2¾oz (⅔ cup) sultanas (golden raisins)
3 tbsp caster sugar, plus extra for sprinkling
1 tsp ground cinnamon
½ tsp ground mixed spice (apple pie spice)
1 quantity of Easy Custard (see page 190)

1. Preheat the oven to 160°C fan/180°C/350°F/gas 4 and grease a 20 x 25cm/8 x 10in ovenproof dish with butter.
2. Generously spread the butter onto the bread slices, then cut them into triangles. Arrange the triangles into the prepared dish, overlapping the slices. As you do so, sprinkle in the sultanas.
3. Mix the sugar and spices together and sprinkle over the top of the bread slices. Pour the custard over the top and allow to stand for 20 minutes, for the bread to absorb the custard.
4. Bake for 35 minutes, or until golden. Sprinkle with extra sugar and serve warm.

RICE PUDDING WITH CARAMELISED PEARS

Serves 4
Preparation time: 15 minutes
Cooking time: 45 minutes

A simple and well-loved dessert that is creamy, comforting and surprisingly light.

120g/4¼oz (⅔ cup) pudding or risotto rice
900ml/30½fl oz (scant 4 cups) unsweetened
    dairy-free milk, plus extra if needed
2 tbsp golden syrup (light corn syrup),
    plus extra to serve (optional)
1 tsp vanilla extract
4 pears, peeled and halved
4 tbsp dairy-free butter
4 tbsp brown sugar

1. Add the rice, milk, syrup and vanilla to a medum saucepan and cook over a low heat for 45 minutes, until thick and creamy. Stir regularly to stop it catching on the base of the pan and add some extra milk, if needed.
2. Meanwhile, preheat the oven to 160°C fan/180°C/350°F/gas 4 and place the pear halves on a roasting tray. Top each one with half a tablespoon of butter and sugar. Roast for 30 minutes, until golden and sticky.
3. Divide the rice pudding into four bowls and top each with two pear halves. Drizzle with extra golden syrup to serve, if desired.

ETON MESS

Serves 2–4
Preparation time: 30 minutes
Cooking time: 2 hours

aquafaba drained from 1 x
    400g/14oz can of chickpeas
    (keep the chickpeas
    for another recipe!)
½ tsp cream of tartar
125g/4½oz (1 cup) icing
    (confectioner's) sugar
½ tsp vanilla extract (optional)
200g/7oz fresh strawberries,
    hulled and quartered
a squeeze of lemon juice, to taste
1 recipe quantity Coconut
    Whipped Cream
    (see page 191)
flaked almonds, to garnish

By now, you've possibly heard of aquafaba – the liquid we normally throw away from a can of chickpeas or other legume. It turns out it makes the most amazing egg white replacer and you can even use it to make meringues! Perfect for one of my favourite British summertime desserts.

1. Preheat the oven to 70°C fan/90°C/200°F/gas ½ and line a baking tray with greaseproof paper.
2. Add the aquafaba to a large bowl and use an electric hand-held or stand mixer to whisk for about 5 minutes until it has more than doubled in size and is white and foamy. Add the cream of tartar and whisk for a further 1 minute.
3. Slowly and gently start adding in the sugar, a spoonful at a time and whisking continuously, until all the sugar is incorporated and the mixture forms stiff, glossy peaks. Stir in the vanilla, if using.
4. Transfer the meringue mixture into an icing bag with a large star-shaped nozzle and pipe into nests. Alternatively, just use a spoon to create mounds and use the back of the spoon to hollow out the centre.
5. Bake for 2 hours. Do NOT open the oven! After 2 hours, turn the oven off and leave them to cool in the oven for at least another hour.
6. Make a quick strawberry purée by blending half the strawberries in a blender with a squeeze of lemon.
7. To serve, layer folds of whipped coconut cream, chunks of fresh strawberries, drizzles of strawberry purée and crushed pieces of meringue into a bowl. Sprinkle over the almonds and serve immediately.

STICKY TOFFEE PUDDING

Serves 4
Preparation time: 15 minutes
Cooking time: 30 minutes

220ml/7½fl oz (scant 1
    cup) unsweetened
    dairy-free milk
100g/3½oz chopped dates
½ tsp bicarbonate of soda
    (baking soda)
115g/4oz (scant ½ cup)
    dairy-free butter, plus
    extra for greasing
100g/3½oz (½ cup) soft
    brown sugar
2 tsp treacle
1 tsp vanilla extract
120g/4¼oz (scant 1 cup) self-
    raising (self-rising) flour
½ recipe quantity Caramel
    Sauce (see page 137), warm
Easy Custard (see page 190) or
    vegan ice cream, to serve

Sticky, sweet sponge cakes, served with a toffee sauce: what could be better? This recipe makes four individual mini puddings, but you could make it as one large pudding, if you wish: it will just need to cook for longer.

1. Preheat the oven to 160°C fan/180°C/350°F/gas 4 and grease four 7.5cm/3in mini pudding moulds or a 1 litre/35fl oz (1 quart) pudding basin.
2. Pour the milk into a small saucepan, add the chopped dates and bring to a boil. Reduce the heat and simmer for 5 minutes, until softened. Remove the pan from the heat, add the bicarbonate of soda and, using a stick blender, blitz to make a purée.
3. In a large bowl, whisk together the butter and sugar until light and fluffy. Stir in the treacle and vanilla, followed by the date purée. Sift in the flour and mix well to combine.
4. Pour the mixture into the prepared moulds, filling them about two-thirds of the way full. Place the moulds on a baking tray and bake for 30 minutes (50 minutes if using the 1 litre mould), until well-risen and golden. The cakes should be shrinking away from the edges of the moulds. Allow to cool in the moulds.
5. Serve the puddings warm with a generous drizzle of toffee sauce on top and some custard or ice cream.

BANOFFEE PIE POTS

Serves 4
Preparation time: 10–15 minutes
Cooking time: 20 minutes

For the banoffee pie
8 vegan-friendly digestive or rich tea biscuits
2 small bananas, peeled and sliced
½ recipe quantity Coconut Whipped
    Cream (see page 191)
dark chocolate, for grating

For the caramel sauce
100g/3½oz brown sugar
30ml/1fl oz (⅛ cup) dairy-free milk
60g/2½oz (¼ cup) dairy-free butter
1 tbsp golden syrup (light corn syrup)
½ tsp vanilla extract
a pinch of sea salt

This is a deconstructed version of the famous '70s British dessert. Simply crush biscuits into a glass, and top with caramel, fresh banana slices and some coconut whipped cream.

1. First, make the caramel sauce. Put the sugar, milk, butter and syrup in a medium saucepan over a medium heat and bring to a boil. Boil for 5 minutes, before reducing to a simmer.
2. Cook for a further 5–10 minutes, until thickened. The consistency should be gooey and runny. Stir in the vanilla extract and add a pinch of salt.
3. To make the pie pots, crush the biscuits and divide evenly between four small glasses. Drizzle some of the caramel on top and alternative between layers of banana slices and caramel until the glasses are almost full.
4. Top each glass with a generous dollop of coconut whipped cream and grate some dark chocolate over the tops, before serving. The caramel sauce can be stored in the fridge for up to 3 weeks. To use again, reheat for 2 minutes over a medium heat so it becomes a more pourable consistency.

RHUBARB AND GINGER CRUMBLE

Serves 4–6
Preparation time: 10 minutes
Cooking time: 30 minutes

For the crumble

250g/9oz (1¾ cups) plain (all-purpose) flour
125g/4½oz (½ cup) dairy-free butter
70g/2½oz (heaped ⅓ cup) soft brown sugar
½ tsp ground mixed spice (apple pie spice)

For the filling

50g/1¾oz (3½ tbsp) dairy-free butter
100g/3½oz (½ cup) caster sugar
1 tsp vanilla extract
3 Bramley apples, peeled, cored and diced
600g/1lb 5oz rhubarb, cut into
    2cm/¾in chunks
100g/3½oz stem ginger preserved
    in syrup, finely chopped
1 recipe quantity Easy Custard
    (see page 190), to serve

Crumble is one of the most comforting desserts with it's soft, tart, fruity filling, buried underneath a sweet, golden, crunchy topping. This twist on the classic adds rhubarb and ginger for a warm kick of flavour and a beautiful pink pop of colour.

1. Preheat the oven to 160°C fan/180°C/350°F/gas 4.
2. Make the crumble topping by rubbing all the ingredients together with your fingertips until you have a dense, sandy mixture. Spread out on a baking tray and bake for 20 minutes until crisp and golden brown.
3. To make the filling, heat the butter in a large saucepan over a medium heat and add the sugar and vanilla. Stir in the apples and cook for 5 minutes until slightly mushy. Then stir in the rhubarb and ginger, cooking until just softened.
4. Tip the filling into a baking dish, and top with the crumble mixture. Bake for 10 minutes, or until golden brown on top and the fruity liquid is bubbling up the sides of the dish.
5. Serve warm with a generous helping of custard.

SALTED CARAMEL APPLE PIE

Serves 8
Preparation time: 25 minutes,
plus chilling
Cooking time: 45 minutes

*If you ever want to jazz up a classic dessert, simply add
salted caramel. As much as I love a classic apple pie, the
caramel in this version takes it to a whole new level.*

1kg/2lb 4oz cooking apples,
    peeled, cored and chopped
    into 5mm/¼in slices
2 tsp ground cinnamon
1 tsp mixed spice (apple
    pie spice)
1 tbsp cornflour (cornstarch)
2 x recipe quantity of Caramel
    Sauce (see page 137)
aquafaba or unsweetened
    dairy-free milk, for glazing
1 tbsp caster sugar
vegan ice cream, to serve

For the pastry
350g/12oz (2 ⅔ cups) plain
    (all-purpose) flour, plus
    extra for dusting
4 tbsp icing (confectioner's)
    sugar
225g/8oz (scant 1 cup)
    dairy-free butter

1. To make the pastry, put the ingredients in a large bowl and
    rub together, using your fingers, until you have a crumbly,
    dense mixture. Add 80ml/2½fl oz (⅓ cup) water, a tablespoon
    at a time, until the dough forms a ball. Turn the dough out
    onto a sheet of greaseproof paper and wrap it up. Refrigerate
    for at least 30 minutes before rolling out.
2. Preheat the oven to 150°C fan/170°C/325°F/gas 3 and grease a
    23cm/9in round metal pie dish.
3. Add the apple slices, spices and cornflour to a large saucepan
    over a medium heat. Stir to combine, then stew for 5 minutes
    until the apples are slightly softened. Remove from the heat
    and stir in half of the caramel sauce.
4. Remove the pastry from the fridge and cut in half. On a lightly
    floured surface roll out one piece to fit the bottom of the pie
    dish. Don't worry about any overhanging bits. Brush the pastry
    around the rim of the dish with a little aquafaba or milk. Fill
    the pastry case with the apple caramel mixture, piling high.
5. Roll out the rest of the pastry to approximately 30cm/12in
    diameter and lay over the apple mixture, pressing the edges
    together to seal. Trim the edges with a sharp knife. You can
    use any offcuts to make decoration for the top of the pie, if you
    like, affixing them with a little aquafaba or milk. Score a few
    lines into the centre of the pie, to allow the steam to escape
    whilst cooking. Brush the top of the pie with aquafaba or milk,
    sprinkle with the caster sugar and bake for 35–40 minutes,
    until golden brown.
6. Leave to cool for at least 30 minutes before serving, so the
    caramel can set slightly. Serve with a scoop of vegan ice cream
    and the rest of the caramel sauce.

Two retro sweetshop favourites, these make great homemade gifts as well.

COCONUT ICE

Makes 20
Preparation time: 20 minutes,
plus setting

225g/8oz (1½ cups) icing
    (confectioner's) sugar, sifted
180g/6¼oz (2½ cups) desiccated
    (dried shredded) coconut
1 recipe quantity Coconut Condensed Milk
    (see page 190) or 250g/9oz of shop-
    bought condensed coconut milk
vegan pink food dye or beetroot juice

1. Line a small 20 x 15cm/8 x 6in baking tin with greaseproof paper.
2. Prepare two mixing bowls and add half the icing sugar, desiccated coconut and condensed milk into each and mix to form a dough. Add a few drops of food dye to one of the bowls and mix into the dough to distribute the colour.
3. Transfer one of the doughs to the prepared tin and use the back of a spoon to flatten it into an even base layer. Add the other dough on top and smooth down, creating a top layer.
4. Transfer to the fridge to firm up and set for roughly 3 hours, then turn out of the tin and cut into cubes. Store in an airtight container for up to 3 weeks.

ENGLISH FUDGE

Makes 20
Preparation time: 5 minutes
Cooking time: 20 minutes, plus setting

1 recipe quantity Coconut Condensed Milk
    (see page 190) or 250g/9oz of shop-
    bought condensed coconut milk
80ml/2½fl oz (⅓ cup) unsweetened
    dairy-free milk
225g/8oz (heaped 1 cup) demerara
    (turbinado) sugar
60g/2oz (¼ cup) dairy-free butter
1 tsp vanilla extract

1. Line a small 20 x 15cm/8 x 6in baking tin with greaseproof paper.
2. Add all the ingredients, except the vanilla, to a large saucepan. Melt over a medium heat and stir until well combined.
3. Bring the mixture to the boil, then reduce the heat and simmer for about 15 minutes, stirring constantly and carefully. Once the mixture reaches 112–118°C/234–244°F (soft ball stage) on a sugar thermometer, remove from the heat.
4. Add the vanilla and beat the mixture vigorously for 5 minutes until it becomes very thick and loses its shine. Press into the prepared tin and smooth down with the back of a spoon. Allow to set for at least an hour before turning out of the tin. Cut neatly into squares or roughly crumble into bite-sized lumps, as you prefer. Store in an airtight container for up to 2 weeks.

BRITISH BAKES

MILLIONAIRE'S SHORTBREAD

Makes 16
Preparation time: 20 minutes
Cooking time: 30 minutes, plus chilling

Buttery, crumbly biscuit base, with an oozy, gooey caramel filling, topped with a hard shell of dark chocolate. The ultimate decadent treat.

For the shortbread base
175g/6oz (1¼ cups) plain (all-purpose) flour
1 tbsp cornflour (cornstarch)
75g/2½oz (6 tbsp) caster sugar
75g/2½oz (5 tbsp) dairy-free butter

For the topping
75g/2½oz (5 tbsp) dairy-free butter
150g/5½oz (¾ cup) caster sugar
75g/2½oz (scant ¼ cup) golden
    syrup (light corn syrup)
2 x 400g/14oz cans of full-fat coconut milk
300g/10½oz dark or dairy-
    free milk chocolate
a pinch of sea salt

1. Preheat the oven to 160°C fan/180°C/350°F/gas 4 and line a 20 x 20cm/8 x 8in baking tin with greaseproof paper.
2. Put the flour, cornflour, sugar and butter a large bowl and rub together with your fingertips until you have a very dense mixture that clumps together into a dough. Press into the bottom of the prepared tin and use the back of a spoon to create a smooth even layer.
3. Bake in the oven for 12 minutes, until golden brown. Leave to cool completely.
4. For the caramel layer, add the butter, sugar, golden syrup and coconut milk to a large saucepan and bring to the boil, stirring regularly. Once the mixture reaches 112–118°C/234–244°F (soft ball stage) on a sugar thermometer, remove from the heat. Alternatively, you can test by dropping a small amount of the mixture into a container of cold water and let it sit for a moment. If it balls together into a pliable, sticky consistency, then it is ready.
5. Pour the caramel onto the shortbread base and allow to cool completely.
6. Gently melt the chocolate in a heat-proof bowl set over a small saucepan of simmering water. Pour over the caramel layer, sprinkle with a tiny bit of sea salt and put in the fridge to set for at least 2 hours before cutting and serving. Store in an airtight container for up to 2 weeks.

COCONUT FLAPJACKS

Makes 12
Preparation time: 10 minutes
Cooking time: 30 minutes

180g/6¼oz (¾ cup) dairy-free butter
6 tbsp golden syrup (light corn syrup)
150g/5½oz (1½ cups) porridge oats (oatmeal)
100g/3½oz (1 cup) jumbo rolled oats
50g/1¾oz (¼ cup) demerara
    (turbinado) sugar
30g/1oz (⅓ cup) ground almonds
50g/1¾oz (⅔ cup) desiccated
    (dried shredded) coconut

Flapjacks always remind me of school bake sales. The smell of freshly baked ones wafted into my nose and carried me towards them, like something out of a cartoon. They're one of my favourite things to bake for a teatime treat, partially because they are so easy.

1. Preheat the oven to 150°C fan/170°C/325°F/gas 3. Line a 20 x 20cm/8 x 8in baking tin with greaseproof paper.
2. In a large saucepan, melt the butter and golden syrup together over a low heat. Once melted, remove from the heat and stir in the rest of the ingredients to combine.
3. Pour into the prepared baking tin and bake for 20–25 minutes, depending on how chewy or crisp you like yours. Leave to cool slightly in the tin before cutting into 12 and serving. Keep in an airtight container for up to 2 weeks.

PARKIN

Serves 16
Preparation time: 10 minutes
Cooking time: 55 minutes

150g/5½oz (heaped 1 cup) self-
  raising (self-rising) flour
1 tsp baking powder
150g/5½oz (1½ cups) porridge
  oats (oatmeal)
2 tsp ground ginger
115g/4oz (scant ½ cup) dairy-free butter
100g/3½oz (½ cup) soft brown sugar
180g/6¼oz (generous ½ cup) golden
  syrup (light corn syrup)
150g/5½oz (scant ½ cup) black
  treacle (molasses)
180ml/6fl oz (¾ cup) unsweetened
  dairy-free milk

*A moist, treacly, ginger cake from Yorkshire,
traditionally eaten around Bonfire Night. Best
served with a hot toddy or mulled cider on a
cold Autumn night.*

1. Preheat the oven to 160°C fan/180°C/350°F/gas 4
   and line a 20 x 20cm/8 x 8in baking tin with
   greaseproof paper.
2. Mix the flour, baking powder, oats and ginger
   together in a large bowl.
3. In a medium saucepan, gently melt the butter, sugar,
   syrup and treacle together over a low heat. Once
   melted, remove from the heat and whisk in the milk.
4. Add the wet mixture to the dry and stir until well
   combined. Pour into the prepared baking tin and
   bake for 50 minutes, or until a skewer inserted into
   the centre of the cake comes out clean.
5. Allow to cool before cutting into small squares. Can
   be stored in an airtight container for up to 2 weeks
   and tastes better the longer you leave it.

MARMITE CHEESE STRAWS

Makes 24
Preparation time: 15 minutes
Cooking time: 10 minutes

2 x 320g/11¼oz sheets of vegan puff pastry
3 tbsp dairy-free butter
3 tbsp Marmite or other yeast extract
4 tbsp nutritional yeast
50g/1¾oz vegan Parmesan-
  style cheese, grated
aquafaba or unsweetened dairy-
  free milk, for glazing

It goes without saying, but you will either love or hate these straws. They have a moreish salty, cheesy flavour, all wrapped up in flaky pastry. Great for serving at parties and get-togethers.

1. Preheat the oven to 200°C fan/220°C/425°F/gas 7 and line a baking tray with greaseproof paper.
2. Unroll the puff pastry sheets and spread one sheet with the butter and the other with the Marmite. Sprinkle the nutritional yeast and cheese onto the sheet with the Marmite and sandwich the other sheet on top, inverting it so that the butter is on the inside, too. Lightly press the sheets together by rolling gently with a rolling pin.
3. Using a sharp knife or pizza cutter, cut the pastry in half lengthways and then into 2.5cm/1in strips along the length – you should get about 12 strips from each half of the pastry. Twist each strip into twirls and place on the prepared baking tray. Brush with a little aquafaba or milk. Repeat with the rest of the pastry.
4. Bake for 10 minutes until puffed and golden. Serve warm, or cool on a rack and store in an airtight container for later on. Best served on the day of baking.

ECCLES CAKES

Makes 8
Preparation time: 20 minutes,
plus chilling
Cooking time: 20 minutes

A British classic originating from Eccles, part of Greater Manchester, these teatime classics are filled with warm, sticky, spiced fruit, encased in a flaky, buttery pastry.

25g/1oz (2 tbsp) dairy-free butter
150g/5½oz (heaped 1 cup) mixed dried fruit
50g/1¾oz (¼oz) demerara (turbinado) sugar
1 tsp ground cinnamon
½ tsp ground mixed spice (apple pie spice)
2 x 320g/11¼oz sheets of vegan puff pastry
plain (all-purpose) flour, for dusting
aquafaba or unsweetened dairy-
    free milk, for glazing
caster sugar, for sprinkling

1. Melt the butter in a small saucepan over a low heat and stir in the dried fruit, demerara sugar and spices. Cook gently for 5 minutes, then allow to cool. Once cool enough, transfer to the fridge to chill.
2. Preheat the oven to 200°C fan/220°C/425°F/gas 7 and line a large baking tray with greaseproof paper.
3. Roll out the puff pastry sheets on a floured surface and use a cookie cutter to cut out eight circles, approximately 10cm/4in diameter. Fill each circle with a tablespoon of the chilled fruit mixture. Brush the edges with some aquafaba or milk and gather on top, pinching to seal. Flip onto the other side and gently flatten.
4. Transfer the cakes to the prepared baking tray. Brush the tops with some extra aquafaba or milk and score three parallel lines across the top with a sharp knife. Sprinkle with caster sugar and bake for 15 minutes until puffed and golden. Allow to cool slightly before serving. Best served on the day of baking.

CARROT CAKE

Serves 8
Preparation time: 20 minutes
Cooking time: 40 minutes

225g/8oz (1¾ cups) self-raising
    (self-rising) flour
1 tsp baking powder
1½ tsp ground cinnamon
½ tsp ground mixed spice (apple pie spice)
225g/8oz (scant 2¼ cups) light brown sugar
finely grated zest of 1 orange,
    plus extra for decoration
100g/3½oz (¾ cup) walnuts,
    roughly chopped
260g/9¼oz carrots, coarsely grated
180ml/6fl oz (¾ cup) unsweetened
    soy yoghurt
150ml/5fl oz (scant ⅔ cup) coconut oil,
    melted, plus extra for greasing
60g/2oz (heaped ½ cup) raisins (optional)

For the cream cheese frosting
100g/3½oz (7 tbsp) vegetable shortening
120g/4¼oz (1 cup) icing
    (confectioner's) sugar, sifted
150g/5½oz (⅔ cup) vegan cream cheese

The origin of the carrot cake is long disputed but it was a popular treat in England during times of food rationing in the Second World War, due to carrot's natural sweetness. Now it is a British classic.

1. Preheat the oven to 160°C fan/180°C/350°F/gas 4. Grease and line two 20cm/8in round cake tins.
2. Sift the flour into a large bowl and stir in the baking powder, spices, sugar, orange zest, walnuts and carrot.
3. Whisk the yoghurt and melted coconut oil together in a jug, then stir into the dry ingredients, mixing until well combined. Stir in the raisins, if using.
4. Divide the mixture equally between the two prepared tins, using a spatula to smooth the tops. Bake for 40 minutes or until a skewer inserted in the centre of the cakes comes out clean. Allow to cool in the tins for a few minutes before turning out onto a wire rack to cool completely.
5. To make the icing, whisk the shortening and icing sugar together, then whisk in the cream cheese a little at a time until you have a soft, fluffy icing. Smooth half the icing over the top of one of the cakes, then carefully sandwich the other cake on top. Use the rest of the icing to top the cake. Decorate the top with some orange zest.
6. Cut into 8 slices and serve or cover with foil and store in the fridge for up to 3 days.

DORSET APPLE CAKE

Serves 8
Preparation time: 15 minutes
Cooking time: 40 minutes

125g/4½oz (½ cup) dairy-free butter,
    plus extra for greasing
225g/8oz (1¾ cups) self-raising
    (self-rising) flour
1 tsp baking powder
½ tsp ground cinnamon
½ tsp ground mixed spice (apple pie spice)
125g/4½oz (⅔ cup) light brown soft sugar
1 large Bramley apple
6 tbsp unsweetened plain soy yoghurt
2 tbsp demerara (turbinado) sugar

*A rustic cake with warm, spiced chunks of apple
and a sweet crunchy topping. Wonderful served
with a dollop of vegan Clotted Cream (see page
106) or Easy Custard (see page 190).*

1. Preheat the oven to 160°C fan/180°C/350°F/gas 4
   and grease a 20cm/8in round cake tin with butter.
2. Sift the flour into a large bowl and stir in the
   baking powder, spices and sugar. Rub in the butter
   with your fingers until the mixture resembles
   breadcrumbs.
3. Peel the apple, cut into quarters and discard the core.
   Slice one quarter into very thin slices and reserve for
   decoration. Dice the rest and stir into the mixture,
   along with the yoghurt.
4. Pour the batter into the prepared cake tin and
   smooth level with a spatula. Use the reserved
   apple slices to decorate the top, creating a flower
   in the centre. Sprinkle the top of the cake with the
   demerara sugar.
5. Bake for 35–40 minutes until a skewer inserted into
   the centre of the cake comes out clean. Allow to cool
   before removing from the tin and serving. Best eaten
   on the day of baking or cover with foil and store in
   the fridge for up to 4 days.

BOURBON TIFFIN

Serves 9
Preparation time: 15 minutes,
plus chilling
Cooking time: 10 minutes

A rich, very-moreish fridge cake with lots of crunch.
This tiffin has been one of the most popular among
my taste-testers – unsurprising, since it is also the
most chocolate-filled.

200g/7oz (heaped ¾ cup) dairy-free butter
140g/5oz (scant ½ cup) golden
    syrup (light corn syrup)
400g/14oz Bourbon biscuits, crushed
30g/1oz (¼ cup) cocoa powder
100g/3½oz (¾ cup) mixed roasted
    nuts, roughly chopped
75g/2½oz (½ cup) raisins
300g/10½oz dairy-free chocolate (I
    use half dark chocolate and half
    dairy-free milk chocolate)

1. Line a 20 x 20cm/8 x 8in square baking tin with greaseproof paper.
2. Put the butter and golden syrup in a small saucepan over a low heat. Allow to melt gently, then remove from the heat.
3. Fold the biscuits in a clean towel or put them in a zip-lock bag and gently bash with a rolling pin to crush them into pieces, leaving some large chunks for a bit of texture.
4. Put the crushed biscuits, cocoa powder, nuts and raisins into a large bowl. Pour the butter and syrup mixture in and mix everything to combine.
5. Transfer to the prepared baking tin and distribute evenly, flattening the top with the back of a spoon. Let set in the fridge for at least an hour.
6. Meanwhile, melt the chocolate in a heatproof bowl over a small saucepan of simmering water. Pour over the biscuit mixture and return to the fridge to set again, for at least 30 minutes. Once set, cut into 9 squares and serve or store in an airtight container in the fridge for up to 3 weeks.

VIENNESE WHIRLS

Makes 8
Preparation time: 30 minutes
Cooking time: 15 minutes

For the biscuits

200g/7oz (heaped ¾ cup)
    dairy-free butter
125g/4½oz (1 cup) icing
    (confectioner's) sugar
310g/11oz (heaped 2¼ cups)
    plain (all-purpose) flour
1 tbsp cornflour (cornstarch),
    mixed with 2 tbsp
    cold water
2 tsp vanilla extract
1 tbsp dairy-free milk (optional)

For the filling

75g/2½oz (5 tbsp) dairy-
    free butter
125g/4½oz (1 cup) icing
    (confectioner's)
    sugar, sifted
about 3 tbsp seedless
    raspberry jam

These beautiful shortbread swirls are sandwiched together with sweet raspberry jam and a light buttercream. It takes a little practise to make them look neat, but it is best to have a few imperfections to prove they are indeed homemade, I reckon.

1. Preheat the oven to 160°C fan/180°C/350°F/gas 4 and line two baking trays with greaseproof paper.
2. Whisk the butter and icing sugar together in a large bowl. Stir in the rest of the biscuit ingredients, except the milk. You want the consistency of a soft paste – if it's too stiff, add in a little bit of milk to loosen it.
3. Transfer the mixture to an icing bag fitted with a large star nozzle. Pipe the mixture onto the prepared baking trays to make 16 circles, starting from the outside, working your way into the centre, trying to keep them all roughly the same size – about 5cm/2in in diameter.
4. Bake for 15 minutes, until lightly golden, then leave to cool completely on a wire rack.
5. Meanwhile, prepare the buttercream by whisking the butter and icing sugar together well.
6. To assemble the whirls, dollop a tablespoon of buttercream onto the flat side of half of the biscuits. You could also pipe it in if you want them neater! Spread a teaspoon of jam onto the other half of the biscuits, then sandwich together and serve or store in an airtight container in the fridge for up to 4 days.

JAFFA CAKES

Makes 12
Preparation time: 25 minutes
Cooking time: 15 minutes

70g/2½oz (⅓ cup) self-raising
    (self-rising) flour
2 tsp cornflour (cornstarch)
45g/1½oz (¼ cup) caster sugar
80ml/2¾oz (⅓ cup)
    unsweetened dairy-free milk
2 tsp apple cider vinegar
2½ tbsp vegetable oil, plus
    extra for greasing
1 tsp vanilla extract
5 tbsp smooth (peel-free)
    orange marmalade
125g/4½oz dairy-free chocolate
1 tsp coconut oil

One of the things that I missed most when I cut out animal products, was Jaffa Cakes, so I was really pleased when I was able to create a vegan recipe that reminded me so much of the originals. These have a spongey base, orange jelly centre and are topped with crisp chocolate.

1. Preheat the oven to 160°C fan/180°C/350°F/gas 4 and grease a 12-hole shallow bun tin with oil.
2. In a large bowl, mix together the flour, cornflour and sugar. Add the milk, vinegar, oil and vanilla and whisk everything to combine.
3. Divide the mixture between the bun tin holes, adding 1–2 tablespoons batter to each. Bake for 8–10 minutes until golden brown, then let cool in the tins.
4. In a heatproof bowl over a small saucepan of simmering water, gently melt the chocolate with the coconut oil. Remove from the heat.
5. Once the buns are cool, place on a cooling rack, over some greaseproof paper and mound a teaspoon of marmalade on top of each one. Drizzle over the chocolate until the marmalade is completely covered.
6. Set in the fridge for at least 30 minutes before serving or store in an airtight container for up to 1 week.

ICED GEMS

Makes 80
Preparation time: 15 minutes,
plus chilling
Cooking time: 10 minutes, plus setting

75g/2½oz (5 tbsp) dairy-free butter
2 tbsp caster sugar
125g/4½oz (scant 1 cup) plain
    (all-purpose) flour

For the icing
5 tbsp aquafaba
250g/9oz (1¾ cups) icing
    (confectioner's) sugar, sifted
vegan food dyes in 4 assorted colours

A nostalgic lunch box classic! These bite-sized treats are so cute and fun to make.

1. In a large bowl, beat the butter and sugar together until soft. Stir in the flour, bringing the mixture together to form a dough. Wrap and chill in the fridge for about 30 minutes.
2. Preheat the oven to 160°C fan/180°C/350°F/gas 4 and line two baking trays with greaseproof paper.
3. Once the dough is chilled, roll it out to ½cm/¼in thick and use a 2cm/¾in cookie cutter or a small bottle cap to cut out the biscuit bases. Transfer them to the baking tray. Bake for 8–10 minutes until lightly golden, then transfer to a wire rack and leave to cool completely.
4. Make the royal icing by mixing the aquafaba into the icing sugar and stirring until you have a smooth, slightly firm icing. Divide evenly into four small bowls and add your chosen food colourings to dye them each a different colour, mixing well for an even colour.
5. Transfer the contents of one bowl to a piping bag with a star-shaped nozzle and pipe a small star onto a quarter of the biscuit bases. Repeat with the next colour until you have four different shades of iced gems.
6. Leave to set and harden for at least 1 hour before serving. Store in an airtight container for up to 2 weeks.

HOT CROSS BUNS WITH MARMALADE GLAZE

Makes 12
Preparation time: 30 minutes,
plus proving
Cooking time: 25 minutes

Not just for Easter, these buns make a perfect breakfast or snack anytime of the year. Toast, spread with butter and enjoy with a cup of tea.

60g/2oz (¼ cup) dairy-
    free butter
250ml/9fl oz (1 cup)
    unsweetened dairy-
    free milk
50g/1¾oz (¼ cup) caster sugar
1 x 7g/¼oz sachet fast
    action dried yeast
410g/14½oz (3 cups)
    strong white flour, plus
    extra for dusting
¼ tsp sea salt
2 tsp ground mixed spice
    (apple pie spice)
1 tsp ground cinnamon
finely grated zest of 1 orange
150g/5½oz (heaped 1
    cup) mixed dried fruit
    and citrus peel
vegetable oil, for greasing

To decorate
25g/1oz (3 tbsp) plain
    (all-purpose) flour
3 tbsp smooth (peel-free)
    orange marmalade

1. In a small saucepan, heat the butter and half of the milk gently until the butter has melted. Remove from the heat and stir in the sugar and the rest of the milk. The mixture should be lukewarm. If too cold, warm very gently and if too warm, allow to cool slightly. Sprinkle the yeast on top and leave for a few minutes, until you see bubbles start to appear on top.
2. In a large mixing bowl, combine the flour, salt, spices and orange zest. Make a well in the centre and pour in the milk mixture. Stir until it comes together into a dough.
3. Turn the dough out onto a floured surface and knead briefly until smooth. Add the fruit and peel, a little at a time, and knead until well distributed throughout the dough.
4. Lightly grease a large bowl with oil and add the dough. Cover the bowl with oiled clingfilm or a clean tea towel and leave in a warm place for 1½ hours to rise. It should double in size. Meanwhile, line a baking tray with greaseproof paper.
5. Turn out the dough again and knead briefly. Divide into 12 equal pieces and roll each piece into a ball. Place the balls onto the prepared baking tray, arranging them in rows to make a rectangle shape in three rows of four buns. Leave about 1cm/½in between each bun, cover with oiled clingfilm or a clean tea towel and leave to rise for another hour. They should expand so that they just about touch.
6. Meanwhile, preheat the oven to 180°C fan/200°C/400°F/gas 6 and prepare the icing. Mix the flour with 2 tablespoons cold water to make a smooth paste that's of a pipeable consistency. Transfer to a piping bag with a 3mm/⅛in nozzle. Remove the clingfilm or tea towel from the baking tray and pipe crosses onto the buns.
7. Bake for 20 minutes, or until well risen and golden on top. Whilst still warm, brush with marmalade for a sweet, sticky glaze. Allow to cool slightly on a wire rack before serving. Store in an airtight container for up to 3 days. They also freeze well.

FESTIVE FEAST

SQUASH NUT ROAST

Serves 6–8
Preparation time: 15 minutes
Cooking time: 1 hour 5 minutes

200g/7oz butternut squash, peeled
   and roughly chopped
1 tbsp vegetable oil
1 onion, finely chopped
3 garlic cloves, finely chopped
1 tbsp balsamic vinegar
1 tsp yeast extract
280g/10oz (2¼ cups) chopped mixed nuts
90g/3¼oz (scant 1 cup) dried breadcrumbs
2 tsp dried mixed herbs
100g/3½oz vegan Cheddar-
   style cheese, grated
40g/1½oz (heaped ¼ cup) dried cranberries
sea salt and ground black pepper

Many vegans are probably sick to death of the nut roast option for Christmas lunch by now. However, this nut roast has a cheesy twist which sets it apart. It's still one of my favourite veggie options.

1. Preheat the oven to 160°C fan/180°C/350°F/gas 4 and grease a 900g/2lb loaf tin.
2. Bring a saucepan of water to a boil and cook the butternut squash for 15 minutes, or until very tender. Drain, rinse and mash with a fork.
3. Add the oil, onion and garlic to a saucepan and fry over a medium heat for 5 minutes, until softened. Remove from the heat, stir in the rest of the ingredients, including the mashed squash, and season to taste.
4. Transfer the mixture to the prepared loaf tin and pat down with the back of a spoon to create a firm mixture, and smooth the top. Bake for 45 minutes, until the mixture starts to come away from the sides of the tin. Allow to cool in the tin for a few minutes before turning out and serving.

SAGE AND ONION STUFFING BALLS

Makes 12
Preparation time: 10 minutes
Cooking time: 30 minutes

1 onion, finely chopped
3 tbsp dairy-free butter
1 tsp dried sage
150g/5½oz (1 cup) dried breadcrumbs
250ml/9fl oz (1 cup) vegetable stock

1. Preheat the oven to 160°C fan/180°C/350°F/gas 4 and grease a baking tray.
2. Fry the onion in the butter for 5 minutes, until softened. Remove from the heat and stir in the sage.
3. Transfer the mixture to a large bowl and stir in the breadcrumbs. Slowly add the vegetable stock and mix until you have a soft but firm consistency. Divide the mixture into 12 portions and roll each into a ball.
4. Place the stuffing balls on the prepared baking tray and bake for 20–25 minutes until golden and crisp on the outside.

BRUSSELS SPROUTS WITH CHESTNUTS AND BACON BITS

Serves 4
Preparation time: 20 minutes
Cooking time: 10 minutes

2 tbsp dairy-free butter
750g/1lb 10oz Brussels sprouts, trimmed and outer leaves removed
200g/7oz vacuum-packed cooked chestnuts
½ recipe quantity Bacon Bits (see page 15)

1. Put the butter in a large saucepan over a medium heat and, once melted, add the sprouts. Stir to coat in the butter, then cook on high for a couple of minutes, to brown.
2. Add 60ml/2fl oz (¼ cup) water, reduce the heat to low–medium, put the lid on and cook for 5 minutes.
3. Remove the lid, crumble in the chestnuts and cook, uncovered, for another minute, until the sprouts are tender and all the excess water has evaporated.
4. Serve the sprouts sprinkled with a generous topping of bacon bits.

CAULIFLOWER CHEESE

Serves 4–6
Preparation time: 10 minutes
Cooking time: 30 minutes

1 large head of cauliflower,
    broken into florets
50g/1¾oz (3½ tbsp) dairy-free butter
60g/2oz (scant ½ cup) plain (all-purpose)
    flour (gluten-free, if needed)
600ml/21fl oz (2½ cups) unsweetened
    dairy-free milk
a good pinch of ground nutmeg
¼ tsp garlic powder
¼ tsp onion powder
2 tbsp nutritional yeast (optional)
100g/3½oz vegan Cheddar-
    style cheese, grated
sea salt and ground black pepper

The side dish I get most excited about is cauliflower cheese. That soft, creamy texture adds a whole new dimension to the meal. Sometimes I add in broccoli too, for some extra green.

1. Bring a large saucepan of water to the boil and cook the cauliflower florets for 5 minutes, until beginning to soften, but still a little firm. Drain the cauliflower well in a colander, then tip into an ovenproof dish.
2. Put the saucepan back on the heat, add the butter and let it melt. Whisk in the flour until it makes a paste, then pour in the milk, a little at a time, whisking continuously to remove any lumps. Keep whisking over the heat for 2 minutes until the sauce becomes thick and smooth. Stir in the nutmeg, garlic powder, onion powder and nutritional yeast, if using, and season.
3. Remove the pan from the heat and stir in half the grated cheese. Pour the sauce over the cauliflower, then sprinkle over the rest of the grated cheese.
4. Bake for 20 minutes until golden on top.

SPICED RED CABBAGE

Serves 6
Preparation time: 10 minutes
Cooking time: 1 hour 15 minutes

1 tbsp dairy-free butter
1 red onion, thinly sliced
2 tbsp light brown sugar
1 tbsp balsamic vinegar
1 tsp ground mixed spice
    (apple pie spice)
1 red cabbage, cored and shredded
2 cooking apples, cored and grated

I love cooking this dish because it makes the kitchen smell so amazing and festive. It takes a while to cook, but it is so simple to prepare and can be made in advance.

1. In a large saucepan over a medium heat, melt the butter and fry the onion for 5 minutes to soften. Add the sugar and balsamic vinegar and cook for a further 10 minutes until the onion is sticky and caramelised.
2. Add the rest of the ingredients along with 80ml/2½fl oz (⅓ cup) water and give everything a good stir. Turn up the heat to bring the liquid to a boil, then reduce the heat to low and simmer gently for 1 hour with the lid on. Check regularly, adding a splash of water if it looks like it is drying out.
3. Serve immediately, or reheat later by adding a splash of water and warming for a few minutes on the hob or in the microwave.

VEGGIE WELLINGTON

Serves 6
Preparation time: 40 minutes
Cooking time: 45 minutes

1 x 320g/11¼oz sheet of vegan
    puff pastry
4 tbsp aquafaba or unsweetened
    dairy-free milk, for glazing

For the pâté
1 tbsp dairy-free butter, plus
    extra for greasing
1 onion, finely diced
250g/9oz chestnut (cremini)
    mushrooms, finely chopped
1 tsp miso paste
1 tbsp balsamic extract
1 large handful spinach or kale,
    washed and chopped
100g/3½oz (scant 1 cup) walnuts

For the filling
1 tbsp vegetable oil
1 onion, finely diced
2 garlic cloves, crushed
1 tbsp balsamic vinegar
1 tsp yeast extract
120g/4¼oz shiitake or chestnut (cremini)
    mushrooms, finely chopped
1 small cooked beetroot, roughly chopped
2 tsp dried mixed herbs
1 x 400g/14oz can kidney beans,
    drained and rinsed
125g/4½oz (1 cup) cooked rice
40g/1½oz (⅓ cup) porridge oats (oatmeal)
4–6 tbsp plain (all-purpose) flour
sea salt and ground black pepper

This is admittedly a bit time-consuming and a little fiddly, but the effort is worth it for that classic Wellington look, with a pink centre, surrounded by mushroom pâté and a crisp, buttery puff pastry casing.

1. Make the pâté. Melt the butter in a medium saucepan over a medium heat and fry the onion and mushrooms for 5 minutes, until softened. Add the miso paste and vinegar and cook for a further 5 minutes, until everything is dark and sticky. Stir in the spinach and leave to wilt. Remove from the heat and put in a food processor along with the walnuts. Blitz to a smooth pâté.
2. Preheat the oven to 200°C fan/220°C/425°F/gas 7 and grease a roasting tray with butter.
3. Next make the filling. Heat the oil in a large saucepan over a medium heat and fry the onion and garlic for 5 minutes, until softened. Add the balsamic vinegar, yeast extract and mushrooms then cook for a further 8 minutes until brown and sticky. Mix with the rest of the ingredients, season and use a masher to combine everything together into a thick, chunky mixture. You can also pulse in a food processor. Shape the filling into a large log shape, the length of the short side of the pastry sheet.
4. Unroll the pastry and spread over a thick layer of the pâté, the width of the log. Place the log on top and cover it with the rest of the pâté. Don't worry if it looks messy!
5. Gently pull the puff pastry up and around the log, tucking in the edges of the pastry as you go so it is completely covered. Seal the two ends together with aquafaba or milk, then turn the wellington over so that the seal is hidden underneath. Brush the whole log with aquafaba or milk to glaze and use any excess pastry to decorate the top and glaze that too. Bake for 25 minutes until puffed and golden.
6. Allow to cool slightly before cutting into 2.5cm/1in thick slices to serve.

CHOCOLATE ORANGE CHRISTMAS PUDDING

Serves 6
Preparation time: 25 minutes
Cooking time: 3
hours 35 minutes

This recipe also makes for an amazingly simple weeknight pudding; just fill four mugs with the batter and microwave for three minutes!

60g/2oz (scant ½ cup) plain
  (all-purpose) flour
3 tbsp cornflour (cornstarch)
2 tsp baking powder
120g/4¼oz (heaped ½ cup)
  dark brown sugar
3 tbsp cocoa powder
150g/5½oz (3 cups) fresh
  white breadcrumbs
½ tsp ground mixed spice
  (apple pie spice)
½ tsp ground cinnamon
finely grated zest and juice
  of 2 oranges (about
  100ml/3½fl oz (scant
  ½ cup) orange juice)
60ml/2fl oz (¼ cup) vegetable
  oil, plus extra for greasing
1 tsp natural orange extract
350g/12oz (heaped 2½ cups)
  mixed dried fruit and
  peel, soaked in 4 tbsp
  brandy overnight
100g/3½oz (¾ cup) pitted
  dates, chopped
100g/3½oz (⅔ cup) dark
  chocolate chips

For the chocolate sauce
100g/3½oz dairy-free chocolate
2 tbsp dairy-free milk

1. Grease a 1 litre/35fl oz (1 quart) pudding basin with the oil and place a circle of greaseproof paper at the bottom.
2. In a large bowl, mix together the flour, cornflour, baking powder, sugar, cocoa powder, breadcrumbs, spices and orange zest.
3. Whisk the orange juice, oil, orange extract and 80ml/2½fl oz (⅓ cup) water together in a small jug.
4. Mix the wet ingredients into the dry ingredients, then fold in the soaked dried fruits, dates and the chocolate chips. Transfer the mixture to the prepared pudding basin.
5. Cut a large square of greaseproof paper and another of foil, both slightly bigger than the basin. Place the foil over the paper and make a 2.5cm/1in thick fold in the centre of both layers. Place on top of the pudding basin, paper-side down, and fasten securely with a piece of string around the basin, under the lip. Tie another piece to this one, run it across the top of the basin and tie the other end to the string on the opposite side of the basin to create a handle, so that you can easily lift the pudding out of the pan.
6. Place a trivet or upturned saucer at the bottom of a large saucepan and place the pudding basin on top. Fill the pan with hot water, so that it comes about two-thirds of the way up the pudding basin. Cover the pot with a lid and bring to a gentle simmer, then let it steam for 3½ hours, checking occasionally and topping up the water if needed so it doesn't boil dry.
7. After 3½ hours, lift the pudding out of the pan and leave to cool for a few minutes, until the pudding starts to shrink away from the basin. Carefully, using a palette knife, loosen the pudding from the sides and turn over onto a plate.
8. Make the quick chocolate sauce. Melt the chocolate in a bowl set over a small saucepan of simmering water and add a few drops of milk to loosen it into a pourable consistency. Pour over the pudding to serve. You can store the pudding in its basin and covered with foil, for up to a year in a cool dark place. To reheat the pudding, steam in the same way for 45 minutes, or microwave for 5 minutes.

CHRISTMAS CAKE

Serves 12
Preparation time: 1 hour, plus
soaking and maturing
Cooking time: 2 hours

600g/1lb 5oz (4½ cups)
    mixed dried fruit
150g/5½oz (heaped 1 cup)
    dried cranberries
75g/2½oz (scant ½ cup)
    glace cherries, halved
100ml/3½fl oz (scant ½ cup)
    ginger wine or brandy,
    plus extra for brushing
180g/6¼oz (¾ cup) dairy-
    free butter
180g/6¼oz (scant 1 cup)
    light brown sugar
1 tbsp treacle
finely grated zest and
    juice of 1 orange
350g/12oz (2 ⅔ cups) plain
    (all-purpose) flour
50g/1¾oz (½ cup) ground almonds
1 tsp ground cinnamon
½ tsp ground mixed spice
    (apple pie spice)
50g/1¾oz (heaped ½ cup)
    chopped nuts
120ml/4fl oz (½ cup) unsweetened
    dairy-free milk

For icing and decoration
4 tbsp smooth apricot jam
icing (confectioner's)
    sugar, for dusting

This is perfect served just as it is, without decorating, but I love traditionally decorated Christmas cakes, with the layers of marzipan and fondant icing. You can also use royal icing (see page 192) to finish the cake.

1. A day, or up to a week, before making the cake, soak the dried fruits in the ginger wine or brandy, giving it a stir every now and then.
2. Preheat the oven to 120°C fan/140°C/275°F/gas 1. Grease and line a deep 20cm/8in cake tin with greaseproof paper.
3. In a large bowl, whisk the butter, sugar, treacle and orange juice and zest together. Stir in the flour, ground almonds, spices and nuts. Slowly mix in the milk until you have a thick batter. Lastly, stir in the dried fruit mixture, along with the soaking liquid.
4. Transfer the batter to the cake tin and smooth the top with the back of a spoon. Bake for 2 hours, or until a skewer inserted into the centre of the cake comes out clean. Allow to cool completely before removing from the tin.
5. Store for up to 3 months in an airtight container and brush the top and sides every week with some extra ginger wine or brandy until you are ready to decorate it.
6. To decorate, warm the apricot jam in a small saucepan or in the microwave. Transfer the cake to a cake board and brush the tops and sides with half of the jam.
7. Generously dust a work surface with some icing sugar and roll out the marzipan to a circle at least

700g/1lb 9oz marzipan
(ensure it's vegan)
1.2kg/2lb 6oz ready-to-roll
white fondant icing
a selection of fruit, such as
cranberries, figs and
candied orange slices
aquafaba, for brushing
granulated sugar, for sprinkling
30cm/12in length of ribbon
sprigs of rosemary, pine cones,
cinnamon sticks, novelty
toppers or anything else
decorative you wish

30cm/12in in diameter. Use a rolling pin to carefully lift the marzipan over the cake and gently smooth down the sides, trimming off any excess marzipan at the bottom edge.

8. Brush the rest of the jam on top of the marzipan layer. Add more icing sugar to the work surface and this time roll out the fondant icing, following the same steps as before, to a circle about 32cm/13in in diameter. Trim the edges neatly and smooth out any marks and bumps with your hands for a smooth finish. Secure the ribbon around the bottom.

9. To crystallize the fruit and the rosemary sprigs, brush each piece with aquafaba and sprinkle with granulated sugar. Set aside to dry thoroughly. Once dry, decorate the top of the cake with the fruit and other toppers.

10. Leave to dry out slightly overnight before serving or keep in an airtight container for up to 6 weeks in advance.

NUTTY MINCE PIES

Makes 15
Preparation time: 20
minutes, plus chilling
Cooking time: 15 minutes

I've had a few people tell me these are the BEST mince pies they have ever eaten. Just sayin'. They are so quick and easy to make, for a last minute festive treat.

140g/5oz (heaped ½ cup)
  dairy-free butter, plus
  extra for greasing
250g/9oz (heaped 1¾ cups)
  plain (all-purpose) flour
1 tbsp cornflour (cornstarch)
30g/1oz (2½ tbsp) caster sugar
a small pinch of sea salt
5 tbsp good-quality, vegan-
  friendly mincemeat
2 tbsp aquafaba or unsweetened
  dairy-free milk
40g/1½oz (heaped ½ cup)
  chopped nuts
2 tbsp icing (confectioner's)
  sugar, plus extra for dusting

1. Preheat the oven to 160°C fan/180°C/350°F/gas 4 and grease a shallow 12-hole bun tin with butter.
2. Sift the flour into a large bowl and stir in the cornflour, sugar and salt. Add the butter and rub it into the flour with your fingertips. Drop in a couple of tablespoons of cold water and bring the dough together. If it is still crumbly, add a little more until you have a firm dough that holds its shape without crumbling. Wrap the pastry in greaseproof paper and chill for at least 30 minutes before cutting out the tart shells.
3. Roll the pastry out on a flour-dusted surface to about 3mm/⅛in thick and cut out rounds using a 10cm/4in fluted or plain round pastry cutter. Place the pastry rounds into the tray and gently pat down the middle. Fill each pastry shell with a generous teaspoon of the mincemeat.
4. Use the excess pastry to cut out star shapes and place on top of the pies. Bake for 10 minutes.
5. Meanwhile, mix the chopped nuts and icing sugar in a small bowl. Remove the pies from the oven and brush the tops with aquafaba or milk. Sprinkle the mixed nuts generously on top. Return to the oven for another 5 minutes until golden brown.
6. Leave to cool slightly before removing from the tins. Sift some icing sugar on top of the pies and serve warm. Store for up to 2 weeks in an airtight container.

GINGERBREAD MEN

Makes 20
Preparation time: 20 minutes,
plus chilling
Cooking time: 12 minutes

Making gingerbread men is perhaps my favourite Christmas activity. The scent of the dough makes me so happy and I love getting creative with the icing designs. These will keep for a couple of weeks (theoretically) so make great gifts too.

150g/5½oz (scant ⅔ cup)
    dairy-free butter
120g/4¼oz (generous ½ cup)
    dark muscavado sugar
60g/2oz (¼ cup) golden syrup
    (light corn syrup)
375g/13oz (3 cups) plain (all-
    purpose) flour, plus extra
    if needed, and for dusting
1 tsp bicarbonate of soda
    (baking soda)
2 tsp ground ginger
1 tsp ground cinnamon
½ tsp ground mixed spice
    (apple pie spice)
1 recipe quantity Royal
    Icing (see page 192)

1. In a small saucepan, gently melt the butter, sugar and golden syrup together over a low heat.
2. In a large bowl, stir the flour, bicarbonate of soda and spices together. Pour the melted butter mixture into the bowl and mix well to form a dough, adding a little more flour if it is too sticky. You should have a smooth, soft dough. Wrap in greaseproof paper and chill in the fridge for at least 30 minutes to firm up.
3. Preheat the oven to 160°C fan/180°C/350°F/gas 4 and line two baking trays with greaseproof paper.
4. Lightly dust a surface with flour and roll out the dough to approximately ½cm/¼in thick. Cut out your gingerbread men with a cookie cutter and transfer to the prepared baking trays, allowing enough room for the biscuits to expand in the oven.
5. Bake for 12 minutes, until golden, then allow the gingerbread to cool completely on a wire rack. Once cool, fill a piping bag with the royal icing and decorate as you wish. Store for up to 2 weeks in an airtight container.

VEGAN ESSENTIALS

CASHEW CREAM AND CHEESE SAUCE

Makes 250ml/9fl oz
Preparation time:
15 minutes, plus soaking

Cashew cream was a revelation for me when I first stopped eating dairy. It is so rich and creamy! Use it to thicken soups and curries, as a salad dressing or make it into the tastiest vegan cheese sauce you've ever tried.

For the cashew cream
150g/5½oz (1¼ cups)
    raw cashew nuts
240ml/8fl oz (1 cup)
    unsweetened dairy-free milk
1 tbsp apple cider or white
    (distilled) vinegar
a small pinch of sea salt

For the cheese sauce
3 tbsp nutritional yeast flakes
1 tsp yeast extract or miso paste
½ tsp English mustard
a pinch of ground nutmeg

1. Soak the cashews in just boiled water for at least 15 minutes, or overnight. Drain the cashews and discard the water they were soaked in.
2. Add the nuts to a high-powered blender along with the milk, vinegar and salt. Add more milk, if needed, to create the desired consistency.
3. To make a cheese sauce, simply add in the additional ingredients and blend together.
4. Use straight away or store in an airtight container in the fridge for up to 3 days.

COCONUT CONDENSED MILK

Makes 250ml/9fl oz
Preparation time: 15 minutes
Cooking time: 1 hour

This takes a bit of time to make but the results are really worth it. Use it for making sweets, caramel and desserts.

1 x 400ml/14oz can full-fat coconut milk
150g/5½oz (¾ cup) caster sugar

1. Pour the coconut milk into a medium saucepan, add the sugar and bring to the boil, stirring occasionally. Reduce the heat and simmer for up to 1 hour, or until the liquid is reduced to a thick condensed milk. Remove from the heat and allow to cool.
2. Use straight away or store in an airtight container in the fridge for up to 2 weeks.

EASY CUSTARD

Makes 700ml/23½fl oz (3 cups)
Preparation time: 1 minute
Cooking time: 10 minutes

It only takes ten minutes and four ingredients to make this warm, sweet custard to serve with your dessert. It's so simple and so good.

750ml/26fl oz (3¼ cups) unsweetened
    dairy-free milk
4 tbsp cornflour (cornstarch)
6 tbsp caster sugar
1 tsp vanilla extract

1. Put the milk in a medium saucepan over a medium heat. Add the cornflour and sugar and whisk together. Continue cooking for about 10 minutes until thickened and smooth, whisking regularly.
2. Remove from the heat and stir in the vanilla extract. Serve warm.

COCONUT WHIPPED CREAM

Makes approx. 400ml/14fl oz
Preparation time: 10 minutes

1 x 400g/14oz can full-fat coconut
    milk, chilled overnight
2 tbsp caster sugar
1 tsp vanilla extract

I always keep a can of coconut milk in my fridge, so I can whip up some of this cream whenever I like. It tastes absolutely amazing and is great for topping desserts and cakes, or serving on the side.

1. Open the can of chilled coconut milk and remove the solid cream that has separated from the water. Add the cream to a large, cold mixing bowl. (Retain the leftover water for a different recipe – it's great in smoothies and curries).
2. Whisk the cream with an electric hand whisk on high speed for 8 minutes until thick. Sprinkle in the sugar and vanilla and beat for a further 1–2 minutes until you have stiff peaks.
3. Use straight away or store in an airtight container in the fridge for up to 3 days. Whisk again before using.

ROYAL ICING

Makes about 650g/1lb 7oz
(enough for 1 large icing bag)
Preparation time: 10 minutes

135ml/4½fl oz (generous ½ cup) aquafaba
500g/1lb 2oz (4 cups) icing (confectioner's)
    sugar, plus extra if needed
1 tsp vegetable glycerine

An essential for decorating gingerbread men or other biscuits. This icing sets just like regular royal icing – you won't know the difference.

1. Put the aquafaba in a large mixing bowl and whisk with an electric hand whisk or stand mixer until foamy. Sift in the icing sugar, a little at a time, and continue to mix for about 10 minutes, until the sugar is incorporated and the mixture is thick and glossy.
2. Add the glycerine and keep whisking until soft peaks are formed. It should now be a pipeable consistency. If you need to make it thicker, add more sugar.
3. Transfer to a piping bag and use immediately or store in an airtight container in the fridge for up to 4 weeks. You will need to whip the mixture again to loosen it up, before using.

VEGAN MAYONNAISE

Makes approx. 400ml/14fl oz
Preparation time: 5 minutes

120ml/4fl oz (½ cup)
    unsweetened soy milk,
    at room temperature
2 tsp white (distilled) vinegar
¼ tsp fine sea salt
juice of ½ lemon
1 tsp English mustard
250ml/9fl oz (1 cup)
    sunflower oil

Vegan mayo is easy to find in the supermarket but sometimes you just can't beat homemade. It is so easy and you can add your own flavours such as garlic, herbs or chilli.

1. Add all the ingredients, except the oil, to a blender and blitz to combine. On medium speed, very slowly pour the oil in as you blend, until you have a thick mayonnaise consistency. It will thicken more as it cools.
2. Transfer to a container or jar and keep in the fridge for up to 4 weeks.

HOT WATER CRUST PASTRY

Makes about 450g/1lb
Preparation time: 10 minutes
Cooking time: 5 minutes

275g/9¾oz plain (all-purpose) flour
a pinch of sea salt
90g/3¼oz vegetable shortening

This makes a nice strong pastry which is perfect for my Porkie Pies (see page 101). You will need to work quite quickly with this dough once you've made it.

1. Put the flour and salt into a large bowl. Add approximately one-quarter of the vegetable shortening and rub it into the flour with your fingertips until it resembles breadcrumbs.
2. In a small saucepan, heat 100ml/3½fl oz (scant ½ cup) water with the remaining vegetable shortening until it has reached boiling point.
3. Pour into the flour mixture and mix with a wooden spoon until it comes together into a dough. Use immediately.

SHORTCRUST PASTRY

Makes approx. 320g/11¼oz
Preparation time: 10
minutes, plus chilling

220g/7¾oz (1⅔ cups) plain
(all-purpose) flour, plus
extra for dusting
a pinch of sea salt
100g/3½oz (scant ½ cup)
dairy-free butter, chilled
2–3 tbsp unsweetened
dairy-free milk

A great all-round pastry for pies and tarts. It's easy to make by hand (cold hands work best) or in a food processor.

1. If you are making by hand, sift the flour into a large bowl and mix in the salt. Add the butter in teaspoons and rub it into the flour with your fingertips until you have a sandy mixture. Pour in the milk, a tablespoon at a time, and mix until it comes together into a firm dough.
   If you are using a food processor, add the flour and butter to the processor bowl and pulse until you have a sandy mixture. Pour in the milk in a steady stream and pulse until it comes together into a dough.
2. Dust a surface with some extra flour and turn the dough out onto it. Knead briefly until smooth. Wrap the pastry in greaseproof paper and chill in the fridge for 30 minutes before using.

INDEX

STOCKISTS

Finding plant-based alternatives to meat and dairy products is so easy nowadays and won't require any trips to specialist stores. Your local supermarket should have everything you need! If you're looking for recommendations, here are some of the best-tasting (in my opinion) ingredients and where you can find them.

If you have a local independent health food shop, then that is even better as they will have more choices and it is always nice to support smaller businesses too.

There is also a website called myvegansupermarket.co.uk which is updated regularly and tells you where to find any vegan food product you are looking for.

Dairy substitutes

<u>Milk and Cream</u>

Alpro Unsweetened Almond Milk

My go-to for baking, cooking and every-day use. A really
  subtle flavour that mixes well with other ingredients.
Available from all good supermarkets.

Oatly Oat Milk

A light, creamy milk which is perfect for
  adding to tea or for use in baking.
Available from all good supermarkets.

Biona Coconut Milk

A full-fat coconut milk which is perfect for making
  whipped cream or for use in curries.
Available from Asda and Waitrose.

Oatly Oat Cream

An alternative for single cream.
Available from Tesco and Waitrose.

<u>Butter</u>

Flora Buttery Spread

My favourite for every-day use and baking.
  Gives a really buttery flavour.
Available from all good supermarkets.

Naturli Vegan Butter Block

Arguably the best tasting vegan butter, plus
  it is zero waste and palm oil-free.
Available from Sainsbury's.

Vitalite Dairy Free Spread

Another option for a good every-day
  vegan butter alternative.
Available from all good supermarkets.

<u>Cheese</u>

Violife Grated Mozzarella Flavour

Melts well in the oven. Supermarket own
  brands offer alternatives now too.
Available from Ocado, Sainsbury's and Waitrose.

ASDA Free From Mature Cheddar Alternative
One of the best tasting vegan cheddar cheeses I've tried.
Available from Asda.

Applewood Smoky Vegan Cheese Alternative
Another good-tasting cheese with a smoky flavour.
Melts really well and comes in slices too.
Available from all good supermarkets.

Good Carma Parmesan Alternative
For topping your spag bol!
Available from Morrisons and Ocado.

Marigold Nutritional Yeast Flakes
Adds a cheesy flavour to dishes or can be used on it's
own as a parmesan alternative. Very nutritious too.
Available from all good supermarkets.

Egg substitutes
KTC Gram Flour
A flour made from chickpeas, also known as Besan. Makes
an excellent egg-replacer, especially for savoury dishes.
Available from all good supermarkets.

Mori-nu Silken Firm Tofu
I sometimes use this brand to make scrambled tofu
"eggs". You can also use any firm tofu and
cook it down with some dairy-free milk.
Available from Sainsbury's, Tesco and Waitrose.

Ener-G Egg Replacer
On occasion, I use this for baking but it also
works brilliantly for Yorkshire Puddings.
Available from Holland and Barrett and Sainsbury's.

Kala Namak (Black Salt)
This is great for adding eggy flavour to vegan dishes
and works particularly well in breakfast food.
Available online from Amazon and Steenbergs.

Meat substitutes
Meet the Alternative Beef Style Mince
My favourite vegan mince but you can also find
supermarket own brands in the freezer section.
Available from Ocado and Waitrose.

Linda McCartney Sausages
There are so many options for decent vegan sausages
now but you can always count on these to be
available almost anywhere and they taste great.
Available from all good supermarkets.

Shopping Online
If you're looking for more choices, there are plenty
of online vegan supermarkets that offer a
wider selection and the latest vegan products
on the market. These are my favourites:

https://www.thevegankindsupermarket.com/
https://www.veganstore.co.uk/
https://www.planetorganic.com/vegan-shop/
https://www.greenbaysupermarket.co.uk/
https://www.alternativestores.com/
https://www.hollandandbarrett.com/

ABOUT THE AUTHOR

Aimee Ryan is the recipe developer, writer and photographer behind award-winning blog WallflowerKitchen.com and author of *Great British Vegan*, where she shares comforting British classics made with plant-based ingredients. She loves experimenting and making a mess in her small Brighton-based kitchen to create the perfect dish. Her work has also been published in magazines and sites such as; *Waitrose Food* magazine, *Waitrose Weekend, Vegan Life* magazine, *Go Gluten-Free* magazine, Great British Chefs, Buzzfeed, HuffPost and Kitchn, to name a few. She has also collaborated with several top brands.

THANKS

Writing my first cookbook was an exciting and daunting task, but all the people below helped me focus on the former and forget the latter.

First, thank you everyone who has bought this book, made one of my recipes, regular readers of my blog and all those who support me on social media, too.

Special thanks to my friend Tess for being an all-round gem and excellent pea-soup-maker. Lots of thanks to my photographer, Jamie and stylist, Becci for the mouth-watering shots in this book and putting up with my messy cooking. Shout out to Chewy for being the best therapy dog. Thanks to Cerys for her encouragement during shoots, Melissa, Charlotte, Jessica, Bella and everyone else at Quarto, who have been really great to work with. Also to Paileen, for the design, Maeve for working with the printers and Pirrip Press for the cover. And a very big thank you to my brilliant agent Tessa for helping make this all happen.

Thank you to my parents. Thank you India, Phillip, Bea, Danni, Helen, Tomás and Marcela for the support. And to Jackie who made the beautiful spoon for me, featured on page 139.